CONTENTS

ABOUT THIS PUBLICATION

This publication has been produced by the International Skills Standards Organisation (INSSO): an independent workforce development consultancy and international standards setting body. We gratefully acknowledge the sponsorship support of Pearson, and the expert advice provided by a number of external stakeholders. However, the views expressed in this report are those of the INSSO project team, and are not necessarily those of any of the people or organisations that have been involved in the production of this publication.

EXECUTIVE SUMMARY

ARCHITECT,
Mumbai

Over the past 30 years a truly transnational labour market has emerged fuelled by globalisation. This has unleashed a variety of forces, including a steady increase in non-farm jobs from 54 per cent of global employment to over 70 per cent today.[1] According to the International Organization for Migration there are 214 million international migrants that have moved to other countries to work, a number equivalent to the population of the 5th largest nation. Quite simply, we live in a world that is constantly on the move. Globalisation, defined as interconnectedness, is not going to stop and the changes in the nature of jobs, technology and the mobility of labour – both now and in the future – will only increase. We therefore have to provide for a fresh proposition for shaping the global workforce, a proposition that is as mobile and transportable as people and one that has a recognisable and usable currency no matter where it is applied. INSSO believes such a currency has been identified: Transnational Skills Standards (TnSS for short).

TnSS have the potential to revolutionise the way we think about labour mobility and how we drive up levels of workforce productivity – which are the main ways a nation grows more prosperous. For years, countries have cooperated to produce Mutual Recognition Arrangements (MRA) of professional qualifications and skills, particularly in the area of immigration-based policy. These have been mainly dual, regional or profession based, but there has never been an attempt to create a common skills currency: a recognisable means of global exchange of skills.

This was something originally called for by the OECD in May 2012, when they produced a *Skills Strategy* calling for skills as 'the new global currency'. INSSO is now taking this one step further from a workforce development perspective by proposing new international standards covering knowledge, competence and proficiency.

Operating as international benchmarks of best practice, TnSS will help shape the workforces of today and the future. At the global level there is the potential of providing easily accessible standards to help individuals, firms, training and official agencies understand what functions are required in order for a particular occupation or trade skill to be carried out to an internationally accepted norm. This includes the specifications of underpinning knowledge and behaviours that are essential if a job function is to be carried out in a productive and creative way. The potential benefits to the global economy and managed migration are immense. Based on in-depth research of an initial number of three globally orientated industry sectors, this report scopes out the potential of TnSS and makes practical recommendations about how they could be developed in the future. We do not claim to have found all the answers to the development of a global skills currency, but we do believe this publication can make an important contribution to an ongoing debate.

CHAPTER ONE – THE GLOBAL SKILLS RACE

Chapter one outlines the profound changes that have taken place in the global economy and how the hidden patterns of trade and the 'common-languages' are exposing every nation to a 'global skills race'. This chapter considers the forces that are shaping skills and workforce development. We argue that the key to winning the global race lies in exploiting the process of human specialisation and exchange, and in nurturing these skills through the new global currency – TnSS.

CHAPTER TWO – A COMMON CURRENCY FOR SKILLS?

Chapter two draws on the findings of research in the IT and IT enabled services, hospitality and tourism, and justice and security sectors, and sets out the case for developing TnSS – a universal set of competency standards, setting a benchmark and developing a common-currency, that will make the global labour market function more efficiently, provide employment opportunities, increase productivity, create wealth and foster the security of our planet. The research illustrates the variety of national approaches to raising standards in these three sectors and highlights the challenges in making effective cross-border comparisons. By identifying and analysing the benefits to the different stakeholders, this chapter makes a strong case for transnational collaboration on skills standards.

CHAPTER THREE – TRANSNATIONAL SKILLS STANDARDS

Chapter three considers what TnSS will actually look like. Again, drawing on the research, this chapter establishes a handful of principles underpinning TnSS; they should describe common functions, not jobs (which vary from company to company across the world); they should describe the outcome of work, not the process (which is covered by local procedures); they should be context-free (i.e. not limited to one jurisdiction), but able to be applied in any country; they should be derived through a consensus of stakeholders; they should be dynamic, responding to external changes and innovations. Three sample TnSS are presented, one from each sector, complete with specifications of the function, its scope and the required behaviours, knowledge and skills.

CHAPTER FOUR – MINTING THE NEW CURRENCY

The final chapter presents a highly practical process for meeting the challenge of gaining consensus on TnSS in a timely way, of how we make TnSS a reality and how we make best use of the resources of all stakeholders. It also outlines the methodologies recommended for the different phases: identification of functions, development, consultation, field-testing and revision of TnSS. The chapter concludes with an evaluation framework to ensure the benefits of TnSS are enjoyed by all stakeholders.

CONCLUSION – BRAVE NEW WORLD

We believe that the future will belong to those countries, industries and organisations whose people are able to deliver sustainable competitive advantage through their skills and their application of productive knowledge. Every economy will want to join the global skills race. The UN estimates that the world population will grow from 7 billion to over 9 billion by 2050, putting huge pressure on our natural resources, but also providing the means for more people to migrate in search of opportunity and work. The central question is how will a more globalised world be better organised? And how can major skills and demographic imbalances be addressed through a more systematic approach to international skills standards like TnSS?

CHAPTER ONE
THE GLOBAL SKILLS RACE

TAXI DRIVER,
NYC

In the last century great powers engaged in a global arms race, two world wars and suffering on an unimaginable scale. In the 21st century, despite contemporary geo-political tensions, and the urgent need to tackle the adverse effects of climate change, the world today is being shaped by human specialisation and exchange, with both achieving new heights in what is becoming known as a 'global skills race'. From Silicon Valley to Shanghai, across the Pacific and Atlantic oceans, this race is helping to supercharge a planet of 7 billion people. This includes a global workforce that, since 1971, has doubled in size to 2.9 billion.[2]

When, in late 2012, Felix Baumgartner climbed up to the edge of space in a helium balloon, the daredevil feat was as much a triumph of technological evolution as it was one man pushing the limits of our biological possibilities. Climbing 24 miles (38 km) into the atmosphere, 'Fearless Felix' as he is known, made his ascent in a balloon with a volume of 30 million cubic feet and a skin one-tenth the thickness of a sandwich bag. Being the first human in history to break the sound barrier in free-fall, his descent took just 10 minutes.[3]

Undoubtedly, there is no inherent need for humankind to jump from the edge of space back down to earth. But the skills, planning and ingenuity that went into such a feat demonstrate just how far we are prepared to push ourselves as a human race, to find fresh areas to specialise in and reach new goals. In Felix's case: through the dangerous sports of base-jumping and extreme skydiving. It is easy to forget – particularly in the blaze of the sponsor's own publicity surrounding the skydive – that the 43 year old from Salzburg had to undertake many hours of dedicated practice training to stand any chance of survival when the final jump came. It's no exaggeration: *training* matters.

'Fearless Felix' is an allegory of the global skills race that is now underway. Nearly every nation is trying to figure out how to expand the boundaries of human potential. It has taken the form of universal rights to a free school education promoted by the United Nations, and the massive expansion in tertiary education that has emerged since 1945. Over the past 50 years, in OECD countries, the number of college educated people with graduate-level qualifications has risen from 13 percent to 37 percent, and current projections suggest this will increase to 50 percent by 2030.[4]

Amongst educators and policymakers a new colloquialism has entered the lexicon: with talk of 'Pisa envy' amongst nations. The Programme for International Student Assessment (Pisa) has been around for some years. The standardised tests target 15 year olds' proficiency in reading, maths and science every three years. The league tables they produce create a flurry of academic and popular interest each time they appear. To be successful like Finland or Shanghai is to sincerely flatter the performance of their education systems. Despite some controversy, testing and standardisation is a fact of life for the vast majority of developed school systems. Used appropriately, testing can be an effective performance improvement and accountability tool. But as *The Economist* magazine remarked on 'Pisa envy': '*The main lesson for policymakers may be to put education at the forefront of the story a nation tells about itself. Countries which do that with conviction and consistency can leapfrog the complacent.*'[5]

HOW BOTH STANDARDISATION AND PERSONALISATION DRIVES GLOBAL GROWTH

The story of the first industrial revolution was one of harnessing the physical power of coal and steel to shift vast quantities of goods by canal, sea and railroad. One of the consequences of this 'annihilation of distance' – as the Victorians referred to the age – was the need to put in place formally un-codified rules about time and space. Indeed, 'railway time' was the first recorded name given to standardised time. In 1840, the Great Western Railway synchronised all station clocks along its routes to 'London time', and within 3 years all the railway companies had followed. Apart from overcoming the confusion of unsynchronised departure and arrival times, the other major reason was the need for safety standards since the growing use of the railways was leading to a number of near misses and accidents.[6] It was the tragic loss of 14 lives in a train accident in the United States in August 1853 that led to the General Time Convention agreed by American railroad companies. Guards travelling on the trains that collided in New England were found to be wearing watches displaying different times.

As the electro-telegraph and mass manufacturing took off during the nineteenth and early twentieth centuries, there was a corresponding development in standardisation and new regulations. From factory clocking-in, shift patterns and accountancy norms, to the growing regulation of trade tariffs and labour standards, the laissez-faire capitalism that symbolised the period was only free up to a point. As Geoff Mulgan points out in his excellent book *The Locust and the Bee*:

'*Global markets work only because legal and other codes are widely adopted, and anyone who tries to export a crate of apples, or a shipload of cars, soon discovers this. Here we find the free market depends upon the rules: standardization has been the motor of growth, with a succession of agreed common languages to make trade possible.*'[7]

In today's global economy we take for granted these 'common languages' and protocols that drive new possibilities in how we interconnect and interact with one another, for both business and pleasure. A network of international organisations now oversees a panoply of standardised rules including the protocols that underlie the Internet (URL, HTML) and mobile phones (GSM). Passenger flights would not be the world's safest form of transportation if it were not for the Safety Management System (SMS) endorsed by the International Civil Aviation Organization (ICAO). The fact that all pilots must be proficient in English in their communications exchanges with civil air-traffic control authorities is just one concrete example of a Transnational Skills Standard that has to be rigorously enforced. There are well over 40 million commercial flights taken each year; only a handful will pass with incident.

International flight codes, bar codes and dialing codes really do bring order in place of chaos. As Lawrence Smith points out: '*this global force owes its existence to a long history of entirely purposeful policy decisions… Many who write about globalization see it as exploding suddenly in the 1970s and 1980s, thus missing the institutional groundwork laid first under Bretton Woods, pressed upon the developing world by its daughter institutions the IMF, WTO and World Bank.*'[8]

In today's world, the growing trend toward personalisation of goods and services would appear to contradict the case for standardisation. Yet without standard operating systems it would be nigh impossible to envisage an international community in which so many multi-national brands, products, supply-chains and business activities could carry on. You can easily make a reservation for a certain type of hotel – even if you've never stayed there before – because you can expect to enjoy some level of service that is commensurate with the published standard or star rating. If these standards either exceed or fall below your expectations then it is possible to take to sites like Trip Advisor, where you can eulogise or complain.

The advantage is that the published standard provides a psychological benchmark – and a degree of consumer confidence – about what to expect in an otherwise asymmetric marketplace. Meanwhile, the hotelier is free to compete openly with other hoteliers – often in the same category – on the basis of expert customer service or some other claim to superiority. Clearly, the hotel you've never visited has rather more scope to mislead you in its official marketing material than if you had been there before: a specific example of asymmetry in the relationship between seller and buyer. The very existence of peer-review sites like Trip Advisor is to redress this imbalance: to help the customer overcome what economists call 'imperfect knowledge'.[9] A central claim for TnSS is that they could assist the global employer, the immigration officer and the training provider, in overcoming their imperfect knowledge in judging whether someone is competent in a specific occupation or trade. At the moment there is no internationally accepted way of overcoming this problem, except through a patchwork set of Mutual Recognition Arrangements between countries, who recognise one another's qualification systems as equivalent to their own. We will look at this in the next chapter.

A similar challenge can be seen in the way crowd-sourcing and crowd-funding is beginning to work. Like all exchange markets, transactions between parties rely on trust. But how do you trust a seller on eBay who lives on the other side of the world and whom you've never met? The answer again comes from standard protocols written into an (online) exchange platform, as well as cultural behavior norms that, to some degree or other, self-regulate and help stamp out abuse. In the case of eBay, it is a peer-activated 'top-rated seller' voting button that separates good from bad customer service. It is this kind of dynamic that will need to be in play as part of any online exchange platform of TnSS. The competencies will need to be benchmarked and verifiable: they should be peer-reviewed and, of course, always aim to minimise fraud or abuse.

Armies of computer programmers – amateur and professional – rely on open-source software platforms that provide users with a cornucopia of bespoke applications. Some of them are free to use while others are proprietary. In this model, the so-called *freemium* economy neatly co-exists alongside a *premium* economy, facilitated by a common language and policing mechanism that coders are able to exploit when developing online products and services. In his seminal book *The Long Tail*, economist Chris Anderson argues that because of the Internet and new technology, it has become possible to eradicate scarcity from many markets, since the once inefficient, or just too expensive to produce, can find an outlet for use or sale. Anyone over the age of 30 can probably still remember when their local record shop or public library had only enough physical space to stock the most popular titles. Choice was limited, so we had to rely on the 'hits' – the products that were most popular and sold the most copies– making the business model of physical retailers viable. Digital stores like iTunes and Amazon have put an end to all that. Indeed, the next revolution in 3D printing may yet put a number of low-cost manufacturing countries out of business since customers will be able to access increasing numbers of 'finished goods' without the need for freight or container shipping. The 3D printer is not without controversy: with the ability to place military technology, like a gun, in the hands of those whom society least wants to have it.

An example of the long tail is the ubiquitous YouTube video that goes viral. Compared to the time of Adam Smith, we live in an age when both the means of production and distribution of exchange have become increasingly *democratised*. What such abundance like this can achieve – thanks to a combination of Moore's Law and Anderson's elongated demand-curve –

is a world of infinite personalisation, products and choices. Such 'niche' products, however, are only made possible thanks to the standardised rules that underpin the global economy discussed earlier. Without these rules and common protocols contained within search and distribution platforms like Google, Amazon, eBay, Netflix, YouTube and so on, many of these consumer choices and cultural pastimes would be non-existent. Similarly, without the common language of skills, captured in some form of competency- and exchange-based mechanism, it will be difficult to see how skills can become the new global currency.

The same is true of our offline world: every time we travel, open up a parcel, engage in social interaction and exchange of one kind or another, we are relying on the collective and codified knowledge of literally thousands of unseen or standardised processes that lie behind our interactions. It is the wiring, if you like, that sits behind nearly every product or service that we consume. What is significant about this observation for the development of TnSS is that many of these processes are ultimately put in place because of the need to train people with the necessary competencies.

Some standard protocols can be routinised and digitised, like dispensing cash from an ATM or paying for services online. Indeed, for some critics of capitalism like Phillip Brown et al., in their book *The Global Audit*, such innovations amount to little more than digital Taylorism which destroys skilled jobs in a global race to the bottom.[10] It is true that technology-based businesses do not create the same volume of employment as labour intensive ones, but the vast majority of customer interactions and global supply-chains will continue to depend on a complex web of human interactions and skills. The challenge for those countries struggling with unemployment is to reform labour markets, innovate in export markets and generally move up the value chain. Ultimately this is a question of changing human competencies and capabilities. The point of this publication is that INSSO has detected a growing requirement to capture these new capabilities in a universal set of competency standards, what we have called TnSS. Chapter 2 explains more about how this might result in the development of a common currency for skills. The remainder of this chapter outlines the forces that are shaping today's global workforce.

THE FORCES SHAPING SKILLS DEVELOPMENT

Gary S Becker is now 82 years old. A Nobel Laureate, he is widely considered the grandfather of human capital theory, even if he did not invent the term. His great insight was to provide an empirical understanding of how investment in human competencies and wellbeing, such as skills, healthcare and the family, produces the kind of return on investment for individuals and societies in comparable ways to investment in capital machinery. In traditional economics it was the factors of production like land and labour that created the surplus value for the owners of them. Yet the productive knowledge – the human capital element – of this contribution to wealth creation was largely ignored. In Becker's model: *'human capital investments tend to respond rationally to benefits and costs'*[11] by ensuring that companies, for example, make investments in their workforce that will maximise a financial or productivity return. Similarly, if governments and individuals invest in their college education – as opposed to stopping or dropping out of high school – Becker empirically showed that better educated people received more of a wage premium, or a return on their investment, over a lifetime than the less well educated. Today, this sounds like an obvious correlation, but in the 1960s, such an idea was uncomfortable for many who thought the idea of human capital was akin to a modern form of slavery.[12]

There are lots of echoes of human capital theory as well as some diversions from it in Lynda Gratton's recent book, *The Shift: the future of work* is already here.[13] For business analysts like Gratton, investing in general education is no longer going to be enough because access to knowledge via Wikipedia and Google will render the *generalist* increasingly redundant. She argues that education and skills systems should seek to encourage the development of individual 'serial mastery' and that people themselves will need to take far more responsibility for self-directed learning and the nurturing of their professional networks if they want to avoid spells of unemployment in future. For workforce experts like INSSO's Tom Bewick, this requires that societies make the transition from knowledge economies – the dominant ideology of the past 30 years – to 'know-how economies', in which far greater emphasis is placed on the development of individual and marketable skills to drive increased specialisation, exchange and real – as opposed to illusory – productivity growth.[14] Dale J Stephens, author of *Hacking Your Education*, provides a more populist view: '*I went to college because I assumed I needed a college degree to get a good job. When I realized that wasn't the case, I left. Thinking back on it now, I went to college because I wanted to do the things I believed that only college graduates could do. Visions of handsome jobs, alumni networks, and all night parties filled my teenage mind. What I realized was that the fantasy isn't the college degree. The fantasy is the path to success a college education is supposed to open. It turns out you can skip college entirely and learn more than your peers ever will.*'[15]

Over the next few decades, policymakers and vocational training systems will need to address at least five interconnected forces in the shifting global demand for employment and skills:

a) Convergence in technology – and what happens when 6 billion people become more easily connected. By 2017, there will be more mobile phones in the world than people. While huge value can be created in some sectors, and new forms of employment can blossom – in other sectors, technology kills jobs.

b) Demographic change – when the youth of India and China will graduate with more degrees than the rest of the world put together; meanwhile by 2050 in the OECD, 1 in 3 citizens will be drawing a pension.

c) Mass mobility and migration – the number of foreign born workers moving across borders stands at 214 million according to the International Organization for Migration; this exponential rise in the free movement of people will continue, as more employers trade in skills, just like merchants trade in commodities.

d) Environmental sustainability – when "green skills" are made more of a reality because the alternative to a future based on fossil fuels is to condemn the planet to intolerable degradation.

e) Human rights and democratic change – as States come under internal and external pressures to reform institutions and labour markets and recognise the right to political participation.

THE FOUR WORLDS OF HUMAN CAPITAL

The global workforce has nearly doubled in 30 years. It has created cheap labour for the global economy and cheap goods for – mainly Western – consumers. It has helped over 1 billion people climb out of poverty in developing countries, while creating ethnic and social tensions elsewhere. In the wake of the Great Recession, some countries are prospering, while others are stagnating. More than 75 million young people are jobless, while 1 billion live on less than $2 per day.

Human capital is the one natural resource that we all have in common. But how do we manage these human resources? What are the challenges facing our world today in terms of education, work and social change?

One way of addressing these questions is to avoid lumping the whole world together. Currently, much of modern labour market analysis is limited, as it tends to ignore the overall societal, economic and cultural context in which skills are developed. A good example of this is the way in which the education sector creates provision by churning out graduates with skills that often bear little relevance to the demands of the real marketplace. Countries need a far better understanding of what is required to exploit their relative productivity advantage in line with the range of socio-economic and demographic forces discussed above. Skills are, at the end of the day, derived from the demands of the real economy in which a particular country or market operates. Demographics, labour force quality and education participation levels, as well as new technology, ultimately guide the supply and demand for skills. Unfortunately, a lot of policymakers still think the causal part of this relationship is the other way round: supply more skills and the economy will grow.

The four worlds of human capital is just one analytical device or way of looking at these issues. They correlate to four geo-political and economic groups of countries, best personified by the G7, the BRICS, MENA and the 'Gazelles'. In reality our four worlds are made up of competing countries and contradictory forces. In some parts of the world immigrants are welcomed with open arms; in other places they are treated with distain. In the rich – 'advanced and ageing' nations – policymakers are trying to square stagnant economies with the politics of migration and the need for growth. The BRICS countries – 'assertive and rising' –face a massive talent gap, potentially acting as a brake on future growth, in part because they are not investing enough in technical and vocational education. In MENA – birthplace of the Arab Spring – the sheer number of young people under 30 looking for work threatens stability in the region and the wider world; and in the Gazelles – 'developing and jumping' – there are some remarkable stories of nations entering the global race with astonishing results.

Figure 1.1 shows our *Four Worlds* in graphic form, from the perspective of median age of their respective populations, the percentage of adults in tertiary education, and GDP per capita at purchasing power parity (2005 prices in USD). Note how the G7 countries are grouped in the top right-hand corner of the chart. These countries share in common ageing populations, with Italy and Japan the group leaders. Compared to the three other Worlds, the G7 also shares high-rates of tertiary education enrolment – greater than 50 per cent. The interesting outlier is Russia, and indeed the BRICS in general, that share more divergences on these measures than most other countries. They might all be '**assertive and rising**', but Russia, for example, is advanced in terms of its tertiary enrolment and the ageing profile of its workforce. Yet, spending power – the relative prosperity of its people – is significantly below that of our '**advanced and ageing**' G7 group. GDP and productivity levels in Russia are generally half that of Europe and the USA. The MENA group is unique because they confirm the opposite of our ageing group, in that they are '**young and changing**'. The median age of most MENA countries is below 35, while tertiary education enrolment rates differ significantly, regardless of whether a country has oil wealth to fall back on or not. Indeed, Israel and Lebanon, both service orientated economies, have the highest education enrolment rates of all. Finally, the Gazelle group of countries show the steady progress they are making, '**developing and jumping**', by sitting somewhere between the BRICS and MENA countries in terms of age profile, GDP per capita and tertiary enrolment. This is the classic profile of lower-middle income countries.

19

Figure 1.2 shows our *Four Worlds* from the perspective of GDP per capita at purchasing power parity (2005 prices in USD), the age profile of the workforce and the size of each country's workforce. What is most apparent here is not only the '**advanced and ageing**' profile of the G7 workforces, but the sheer size and contribution of the BRICS, particularly India and China, to the global talent pool. The MENA countries hardly register in terms of workforce size, yet, this chart confirms the extent to which these countries are still '**young and changing**.' Many of the Gazelle countries are catching up with the G7 in terms of labour force size, although still have a significant way to go in terms of rising levels of income.

Both these charts raise pertinent questions about the source of rising living standards in future unless both improvements in living standards, combined with the freer movement of international migrants, is made more possible.

FIGURE 1.1 FOUR WORLDS OF HUMAN CAPITAL: TERTIARY ENROLMENT AND MEDIAN AGE (2009)

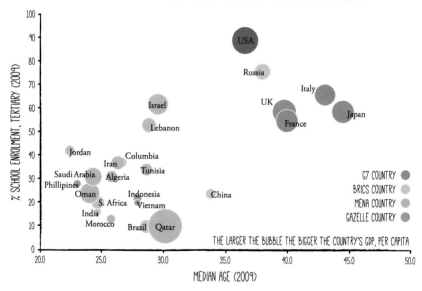

Figure 1.1: Shows the x-axis as median age; the y-axis as the percentage of school enrolment, and the z-axis (the size of the bubbles) represents a country's GDP, per capita, PPP (constant 2005, international $) (the bigger the GDP, the larger the bubble); Country analysis: x axis = median age; y-axis = percentage of school enrolment; z-axis = GDP, per capita, PPP; Analysis of Canada is not included in Figure 1.1 as the latest data for school enrolment, tertiary (% gross) is from 2002. Sources of data listed in the Research Methodology Annexe.

FIGURE 1.2 FOUR WORLDS OF HUMAN CAPITAL: GDP PER CAPITA AND MEDIAN AGE (2009)

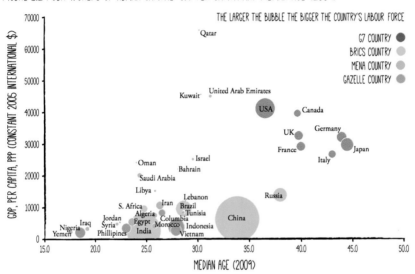

Figure 1.2: Shows the x-axis as median age; the y-axis as the country's GDP and the z-axis (the size of the bubbles) represents a country's labour force (the bigger the labour force, the larger the bubble); Country analysis: x-axis = median age; y-axis = GDP, per capita, PPP; z-axis = labour force. Sources of data listed in the Research Methodology Annexe.

The four worlds of human capital are reshaping our planet, which will have major implications for decades to come.

1. THE ORIGINAL G7 NATIONS: USA, CANADA, GERMANY, FRANCE, ITALY, JAPAN AND THE UK 'ADVANCED AND AGEING'

These are the nations that helped rebuild the global economy after the Second World War. Until recently, they have accounted for over 60 per cent of world GDP. Migrants have accounted for over 40 per cent of labour force growth in these advanced nations, helping to fuel their economies. Advanced countries, like the G7, have been the first to transition from heavy manufacturing to serviced based economies: losing 20 million factory jobs since 1980. While per capita incomes are the highest for this group of countries, income inequality has become the most extreme since the mid-1970s, as median to low-paid workers have not shared as much in the benefits of growing prosperity. Income polarisation between rich and poor is rife. In the future, 40 per cent of expected retirees will be in advanced countries, while the demand for un-skilled labour will collapse. Even with advances in technology, a falling or stable birth rate and ageing workforce is likely to put severe pressure on these countries to innovate (i.e. sustain value in trading products and services) and/or open up to more immigration, particularly to support the retired population. Potentially, this is a demographic, political and skills time bomb. That is why we refer to these countries as: '**advanced and ageing**'.

2. THE BRICS: BRAZIL, RUSSIA, INDIA, CHINA AND SOUTH AFRICA 'ASSERTIVE AND RISING'

The term BRIC, the acronym denoting Brazil, Russia, India and China and now including South Africa; was first coined by Jim O'Neil, an economist, in 2001. Since then this group of countries has gone on to have a profound impact on the global economy, particularly the rise of India and China as economic and population powerhouses. This group shares as many divergences as it does common features. On the one hand, the BRICS are emerging, increasingly plugged into trade throughout the global economy, but they also share many different socio-economic and political traditions. India is the world's largest (capitalist) democracy. China is the world's largest (state-capitalist) officially communist one-party state. Organised crime and corruption is a problem to varying degrees, while Russia – in terms of educational attainment levels – shares many characteristics with the advanced and ageing group. However, the BRICS are increasingly a powerful trading block, recently agreeing to set up their own development bank and collaborative institutions. These countries are characterised as "**assertive and rising**" because they are already starting to eclipse the G7 as the main drivers of global growth, jobs and numbers of graduates. Paradoxically, however, all these countries face a huge productivity challenge. The reforms enacted, in many cases, are simply not keeping pace with the growing demand on these populations to produce high-value added goods and services. Nor are enough labour intensive industries like social welfare services being created. India, for example, has added 67 million non-farm jobs in the last decade, but only enough to keep pace with labour force growth.[16] China is increasingly ageing, so will likely have to encourage outside immigration – potentially a challenge to internal security. Russia is facing a decline in overall population. The other countries face similar challenges, not least to avoid social tensions boiling over because of entrenched poverty and unemployment.

3. MENA (MIDDLE EAST AND NORTH AFRICA): EGYPT, TUNISIA, SAUDI ARABIA, ISRAEL, LEBANON AND 18 OTHER STATES. 'YOUNG AND CHANGING'

MENA stands for Middle East and North Africa. These countries are mainly Islamic, although countries like Egypt and Lebanon are more secular and Israel is a Jewish state. The Arab Spring has affected a number of countries since 2010, with unfinished revolutions still unfolding, particularly in places like Syria. Some countries, like Saudi Arabia and Qatar, are hugely oil-rich, while others, like Lebanon, depend on smaller industries, tourism and service exports for income. Whilst Israel has high-levels of entrepreneurship. What nearly all these countries have in common is demographics: up to two-thirds of their populations are under the age of 30. Youth unemployment is very high – 50 per cent in most cases. While college enrolment rates have increased significantly, these economies are failing badly at creating enough college-level service sector jobs. Religion and culture are other major factors in the Arab world, where women's participation in the labour market is below 15 per cent of the workforce in some cases. Rich economies, like Saudi Arabia, are very dependent on oil exports and cheap immigrant labour. Indigenous workers opt for cushy jobs in the public sector. MENA countries will need to diversify their industrial base in the years to come, as the global economy shifts to cleaner sources of energy. Tertiary education is prized in the Arab World, but employers complain of a major mismatch in what courses and curricula provide and the requirements of industry. For example, 5 million students graduated from university in Egypt between 1995 and 2006; yet only 1.8 million graduate level jobs were created. These are some of the antecedents of the Arab Spring in the region and the cause of social unrest. That is why we describe these countries as '**young and changing**'.

4. GAZELLES: E.G. NIGERIA, SINGAPORE, VIETNAM, PHILIPPINES, BANGLADESH, AFGHANISTAN AND INDONESIA 'DEVELOPING AND JUMPING'

We call this group of countries Gazelles because they are either developing or were previously developing, and some have made great strides relatively recently. They include a diverse array of nations. Some, like Indonesia, are highly populated and share a lot in common with the BRICS. Nigeria's economy benefits in similar ways to the oil-rich countries of MENA, yet poor primary education, healthcare and high crime stultify growth. On the positive side, Vietnam has reduced the number of farm jobs from two-thirds of the labour force, to less than half, creating 12 million new service-orientated and manufacturing jobs in recent years. The Philippines created 3.5 million service jobs between 2000 and 2010, mainly in IT and IT enabled related sectors. Singapore is a city-state that is lauded the world over for its human capital policies; going from a poor Colonial local port to a modern open economy within a generation, creating per capita incomes higher than the United States. Some of these countries are also benefiting from a 'demographic dividend' brought about by skilled young people joining the labour market, along with their attractiveness as a location for low-cost, labour intensive industries. That's why we call these economies Gazelles: '**developing and jumping**'.

TALENT WARS TO COME

Looking at the global skills race through the lens of our four worlds of human capital highlights a number of portents about the future. The first observation is that the advanced and ageing societies – whatever the difficulties politically of opening up to migrants – will increasingly find it difficult to afford the social welfare provision they've become used to unless they can reduce the dependency ratio and boost productivity. Enabling more skilled immigration, not less, is one solution. The fight against stagnation will prove a tall order – as Japan has found – since young people in plentiful supply will almost always reduce the dependency ratio and give countries both a dynamic and productive technological base on which to grow. Perhaps the biggest story of the next decades will be what the BBC economics commentator, Paul Mason, calls the 'graduates with no future' phenomenon. This is pronounced in some advanced countries more than others and was originally associated with the Arab Spring. But it is clear from the data, that the traditional method of supplying skilled workers from the enlargement of higher education is being challenged from the bottom-up. The USA and to a lesser extent, the UK, is amongst the first of the G7 countries to see university enrolments decline in recent years. Yet paradoxically all the advanced and ageing countries will continue to see major skills shortages in jobs requiring ingenuity, technical ability and raw talent. Meanwhile, the lower skilled will see their take-home pay squeezed even further, even if the doom-mongers, those who argue that these unskilled jobs will completely disappear, may be proven wrong.

The BRICS may dominate the economic landscape in the next 50 years because of their massive populations and financial clout in world markets. But they may also encounter the most global tensions of our four worlds, for the simple reason that the quality of the workforce and its labour mobility across borders will be amongst the biggest socio-economic challenges they face. For example, India set a target in its National Skill Development Mission of 2007 to skill-up some 500 million people in the working age category by 2022.[17] There are already indications that this target would pose a significant challenge to achieve. The other BRICS – like China – are seeing commencement of transitioning to a service economy, and with it rapidly rising wage expectations, placing a strain on the very model that has delivered an economic miracle thus far. Brazil, Russia and South Africa will continue to deal with the legacy of grinding poverty, corruption and some extremely unproductive parts of their economies. Russia, for instance, has half the labour productivity that the European Union had in 2010. Like the challenges of so many middle-income countries, the BRICS are no different.

The MENA countries face a different set of challenges. It is hard to predict the outcome of the Syrian civil war or whether the Arab Spring will take another turn. What is clear is that the MENA countries do not have time on their side when it comes to the demographic time bomb that sits beneath them.

Whatever the macroeconomics of these developments, the social contract at work will continue to change. Bruce Tulgan in *Winning the Talent Wars* describes these changes as a shift from a feudal labour market to one based on free agents.[18]

CONCLUSION

To understand the massive changes going on in the global economy today it is hard to ignore the human capital dimension. In amongst the dry statistics about increases in trade and capital flows there's an age-old story. For millennia, societies became rich because they got smart. The difference now is that specialist knowledge and access to world markets is no longer the preserve of a privileged few. The hidden patterns of trade and the common-languages that power these flat platforms are exposing every nation in a global skills race. For the education systems that respond to this challenge there will be no limit to future growth. The key to winning the global race lies in nurturing these skills and competencies as the new global currency. The next chapter will examine whether this currency is achievable and what frameworks might be put in place.

CHAPTER TWO

A COMMON CURRENCY FOR SKILLS?

PHOTOGRAPHER,
Beijing

The King of Lydia, Croesus, is generally credited with inventing the first common currency. In the fifth century BC, free exchange was made possible because of the rudimentary coins that Lydia minted. They would in time be more refined – based on gold – and translate to a widely accepted store of value to be exchanged for chattel. To this day, to be "rich as Croesus" is a synonym for a wealthy person.

As discussed in chapter one, the global labour market depends on forms of specialisation and exchange. Prosperity is driven by a nation's (free) trade and its relative productivity advantage. The source of that advantage is human capital. It led the OECD – a group of leading nations – to declare in May 2012: 'skills are the new global currency.' Like the coinage of today, however, currencies – whether financial or skills related – can lose value, particularly if they become debased. The OECD had this to say:

'Skills have become the global currency of 21st-century economies. But this "currency" can depreciate as the requirements of labour markets evolve and individuals lose the skills they do not use. For skills to retain their value, they must be continuously developed throughout life. Getting the best returns on investment in skills requires the ability to assess the quality and quantity of the skills available in the population, determine and anticipate the skills required in the labour market, and develop and use those skills effectively in better jobs that lead to better lives. Working towards achieving this is everyone's business: governments, employers, employees, parents and students need to establish effective and equitable arrangements as to who pays for what, when and how.'[19]

If there were ever a convincing argument for the introduction of TnSS, it is contained in such words. The main challenge for TnSS therefore is one of understanding how to 'assess the quality and quantity of skills available' together with developing the exchange based mechanism – something all currencies depend upon – 'to use those skills effectively in better jobs that lead to better lives.'

The remainder of this chapter is concerned with why we need a new currency for skills and how that might work. Crucially, what are the skills that lend themselves to such exchange? And what principles should underpin any common currency leading to the introduction of some kind of Transnational Skills recognition? To understand that challenge, we also need to review what has been done already. Drawing on research commissioned by INSSO for this publication, the chapter will examine the issue of a common currency for skills through the lens of three industry sectors: IT and IT enabled services; security and justice; and hospitality and tourism.[20]

One of the first points to clarify is what we mean by exchange. Unlike goods, human capital is not exchanged in quite the same way. Indeed, the treatment of human beings as chattel is nothing more than slavery. Labour markets globally are far from perfect. All sorts of impediments get in the way of efficiency. Rights at work and job protection for some groups depend on a whole host of political norms. Unlike the common languages that underpin the workings of the Internet, there is no such universal language around cross-border skills recognition, other than a handful of mutual recognition and cross-national qualification frameworks. These are discussed in more detail below, after an explanation of what skills might be most suitable for the notion of exchange.

FUNGIBLE, TRADABLE AND UNIQUE SKILLS

The key to understanding what skills can be exchanged is described in Figure 2.1. In undertaking our research we discovered that current labour market classifications are unhelpful when it comes to assessing whether skills are exchangeable or not. In fact, most countries' classification of skills are almost entirely driven by attainment levels in education or linked to a proxy-form of currency, like qualifications. That tells you something about certification, but it provides very little in terms of whether a particular skill is transnational.

To understand which skills are transnational, and therefore more easily exchangeable, we have developed a schema that explains some of the occupations that are more likely to be accessible to TnSS.

The inverted pyramid operates down a central spine and explains the extent to which global labour markets operate on the basis of 'open systems of exchange,' or they are inhibited by 'closed systems of exchange.' Where open systems of exchange are evident – driven by changes in technology like e-commerce, free trade, or encouraged migration – then we describe these skills as either fungible or tradable.

Skills are fungible in our schema, such as a call centre operator, because the role can be performed almost anywhere in the world, by almost anyone, provided the person receives the appropriate training. Similarly, there are many skills – particularly in the skilled trades and professional occupations – that are not fungible in the strictest sense, but are nevertheless tradable, provided countries operate an open system of exchange in those occupations. A good example is the skills shortage occupational lists that countries like Australia, Canada and the UK operate when assessing applications for work visas from potential migrants.[21]

Clearly, the biggest barrier to open systems of skills exchange rest in a number of factors, not least specific laws, regulations and immigration policies that prevent the free movement of people.

But even if the existence of these controls were fully lifted, there would still be certain skills and occupations that are the opposite of fungible: they are unique. A good example of such a unique skill or role is where 'star quality' is evident, like a professional athlete. The election of a new Pope, by the cardinals' conclave, is probably one of the most exclusive occupational global labour markets in the world. While a Pope can technically come from anywhere, only one person (until recently at least) can be Pope! Unlike our call centre operator example, there is very little demand for an exchange market in Popes. This is already addressed through a closed system of exchange: the Papal Conclave.

From a TnSS point of view, what does this tell us? We believe it shows that a large proportion of skills and occupations in the global economy are exchangeable. Indeed, the impact of globalisation in recent years has led to a large proportion of occupational and skills markets to become, in the words of Thomas L Friedman in his seminal book, *The World is Flat*, fungible.

The issue of which occupations to develop TnSS for will be driven to a large extent by whether or not the skills demanded by industry are fungible or tradable or on the cusp of this market at some undefined point within in Figure 2.1 noted as the 'porous zone'. A good example of a skill set in the porous zone is the role of CEO. Just because many economies have CEOs, it does not follow that every CEO has a set of tradable skills. CEOs do not require TnSS because global recruitment consultants already have the appraisal mechanisms to determine which types of leadership skills are exchangeable and which are unique to the person's previous job role. The CEOs of large investment banks tend to move around because high finance and capital flows (operating in open exchange markets) are truly global.

FIGURE 2.1 TRANSNATIONAL SKILLS: FROM FUNGIBLE TO UNIQUE

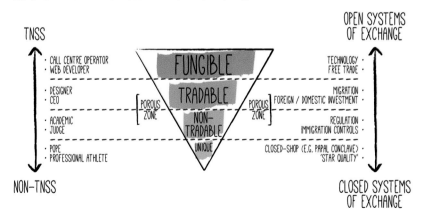

DRIVERS FOR A COMMON SKILLS CURRENCY

The three sectors selected for in-depth research – IT and IT enabled services, justice and security, and hospitality and tourism – have a high percentage of fungible skills which can be performed anywhere in the world (e.g. call centre operators, cybercrime experts, travel website designers) and tradable skills which can be transported to other global destinations (e.g. IT network engineers, security guards, hotel receptionists). They are sectors already characterised by high levels of offshoring, labour migration and international collaboration.

The research sought both to understand the ways in which different countries describe the competences, knowledge and skills workers require, and also to gauge the appetite for a common expression, or "common currency", for skills. Numerous examples of national definitions of workplace skills were discovered, as well as a few international classifications, particularly in the IT sector. The research also revealed a handful of very strong drivers for a common currency of skills.

RISING GLOBAL EXPECTATIONS

Today, no country's economy functions in isolation. Every nation's agriculture, industry and, especially, service sector competes in a global marketplace. Whilst local traditions remain, increasingly organisations need to adopt and adapt global best practices and modern technology in order to remain competitive. This means that the functions performed, and the skills workers need to perform them, are becoming increasingly similar across the globe. The job roles of waiters, software developers or prison guards throughout the world, are practically identical, once allowance has been made for local customs and regulations.

We have become accustomed to customer charters and international kitemarks (such as ISO 9001) and we expect work to be delivered to certain standards. As individuals, we insist on certain standards of service to be provided by receptionists in a hotel or waiting staff in a restaurant; if these standards are not met we take our custom elsewhere, either to another establishment or a different resort altogether (and we let the world know of our experience through Trip Advisor). Traditionally, organisations have trained their in-house workforce to deliver goods and services to their own standards; today, they can choose to outsource work, such as software development or IT helpdesk support, to any organisation in the world which can guarantee the same quality of output. A common currency of skills would facilitate compliance with these standards. In the justice sector, it would also help those nations wishing to improve their human rights record to train guards to treat prisoners in line with international standards of custodial care.

LABOUR SUPPLY AND DEMAND

In the sectors studied, there have been significant increases in demand for workers with relevant skills. The current skills gaps and mismatches are likely to be exacerbated if they are not addressed on a global basis.

The Indian IT-BPM sector is a world-renowned success story, with direct employment increasing nearly seven-fold in the first decade of this century, from 430,000 in 2000-1 to nearly 3 million in 2012-13 (with indirect employment estimated at a further 9.5 million). This huge workforce is meeting a global demand for IT and BPM (over 70 per cent of revenues come from exports) without travelling out of the country. However, this level of growth would be unsustainable without significant internal migration (the city of Bangalore, for example, grew from 5 million to 8.5 million in the same period) and substantial investment in educational initiatives to prepare a talent pipeline for the Indian IT industry.

India, along with other Asian countries, is a significant exporter of workers to fill skills gaps in other countries such as the Gulf States. This pattern is repeated throughout the world with workers migrating from countries with high unemployment to countries where there are labour shortages. The problem faced by employers when recruiting from abroad, and governments when setting immigration policy, is understanding and validating the competences of prospective immigrant workers. Having a common currency of skills could alleviate this problem, or at least a common exchange mechanism like the European Qualifications Framework (which is already gaining recognition outside Europe).

TACKLING INTERNATIONAL CRIME

Our research in the justice and security sector revealed the need for a single set of descriptors for the competence, knowledge and skills needed to tackle international crime, particularly human trafficking and cybercrime.

Human trafficking is the dark side of meeting the demand for labour, where men, women and children are forced into performing services or other work against their will, in a form of modern-day slavery. Although some human trafficking is internal, such as debt bondage in many countries, most occurs across international borders and requires a consistent and coordinated approach. Whilst there are some standards developed by individual border agencies ensuring detection and arrest of perpetrators, a significant reduction in human trafficking may only be achieved by source, transit and destination countries adopting a common set of standards ensuring not just detection and arrest, but also prevention and prosecution and involving a wider range of agencies (e.g. schools, health services and social services).

Cyberspace, by definition, recognises no national boundaries and governments are concerned that criminals, terrorists, foreign intelligence services, foreign militaries and politically motivated "hacktivists" may choose to attack vulnerabilities in institutional or individual cyber-defences. The UK Government's Cyber Security strategy, for example, sets out four objectives:

1. to tackle cyber crime and be one of the most secure places in the world to do business in cyberspace
2. to be more resilient to cyber attacks and better able to protect our interests in cyberspace
3. to have helped shape an open, stable and vibrant cyberspace which the UK public can use safely and that supports open societies
4. to have the cross-cutting knowledge, skills and capability it needs to underpin all our cyber security objectives.

Whilst there are competitive and diplomatic issues involved here, it would clearly make sense for allies to work together to define the "cross-cutting knowledge, skills and capability" required to tackle cybercrime and to pool resources to develop them.

MARKET EFFICIENCY

There are significant economies of scale to be enjoyed by developing transnational rather than national definitions of competences, knowledge and skills. The main English-speaking countries covered by our research have each invested substantially in developing Vocational Education and Training systems based on their own definitions; all are very similar to each other. A single, transnational set of definitions could be achieved at a fraction of the cost, and would place such definitions within the grasp of poorer nations.

Economies of scale could also be achieved in the provision of learning; common standards across the world would mean that education and training providers would be able to access a much wider market over which to amortise the costs of developing their courses and learning products. Learners would be assured of the international currency of their learning and qualifications, based on common Transnational Standards.

BENCHMARKING

A common currency for skills should not imply that work is performed in exactly the same way throughout the world; there will always be room for local practices and regulatory requirements. As we travel throughout the world, unless we only visit global fast-food outlets, we hope to experience the flavours of traditional menus or modern dishes concocted by creative chefs; however, we also expect that international standards of food hygiene be applied.

TnSS should not be seen as a straightjacket, but as a benchmark, against which local employers can measure the quality of their workers' performance. Employers and their staff can identify the competence, knowledge and skills that they share in common with others throughout the world and also specify those elements that make their work distinctive. When hiring workers with TnSS credentials from the other side of the world, employers can be assured that their performance will meet the international standard. They will also be clear about what they need to learn on the job to give their work that competitive edge.

In summary, this common currency of TnSS is conceptualised to make the labour market function more efficiently, provide employment opportunities, increase productivity, create wealth and foster the security of our planet. National skills systems have played a vital role in the upskilling of local workforces and national competitiveness. However, they are now in danger of becoming the equivalent of tariff barriers to the free movement of labour. It might be time to draw up the equivalent of a GATT agreement on a universal currency for skills. An approach like this would put the management of skilled migration on the same international footing as transnational trade and the significant efforts that go into regulating global finance.

WHAT SKILLS CURRENCIES ARE IN USE TODAY?

Many countries and regions have developed their own systems for defining, classifying and valorising the competences, knowledge and skills used at work. These "skills currencies" are variously called *Assessment Standards* (New Zealand), *Competency Standards* (Asia-Pacific Region, China), *National Occupational Standards* (UK), *Professional Standards* (Quebec), *Qualifications Standards* (Australia), *Skills Standards* (Texas), *Units of Competence* (UK) and *Unit Standards* (New Zealand, South Africa). Our research for this publication has been limited to standards available in the English language and in the three sectors of hospitality, IT, and justice and security.

To illustrate the similarities and differences between standards defined in different jurisdictions, five sample standards have been compared, all covering broadly the same function: *Interact with IT clients* (Australia), *Deal remotely with basic IT service requests/incidents* (India), *Resolve computer users' problems* (New Zealand), *Resolve computer users' problems* (South Africa), *Carry out designated 'IT Service Help Desk and Incident Management' activities under supervision* (UK). IT helpdesk support has been selected as it is clearly a function that can be delivered anywhere in the world as long as the IT user and the helpdesk worker are able to communicate effectively in a common language.

Although the language used in the standards is different (the Australian, Indian and UK examples speak directly to the worker, whereas their New Zealand and South African counterparts use the passive voice familiar in standards used in quality assurance systems), the performance requirements of these standards are very similar. There appears, therefore, to already be a high level of consensus in the IT industry about what is expected of those responding to users' requests at the IT helpdesk.

FIGURE 2.2 COMPONENTS OF STANDARDS FROM 5 NATIONS

	AUSTRALIA	INDIA	NEW ZEALAND	SOUTH AFRICA	UK
REFERENCE NUMBER	Y	Y	Y	Y	Y
TITLE	Y	Y	Y	Y	Y
DESCRIPTOR / DESCRIPTION / PURPOSE	Y	Y	Y	Y	Y
ELEMENTS / OUTCOMES / SPECIFIC OUTCOMES	Y	N	Y	Y	N
PERFORMANCE CRITERIA / ASSESSMENT CRITERIA / EVIDENCE REQUIREMENTS	Y	Y	Y	Y	Y
KNOWLEDGE	Y	Y	N	Y	Y
SKILLS / UNDERSTANDING HOW TO	Y	Y	N	Y	Y
RANGE / SCOPE / EXPLANATORY NOTES	Y	Y	Y	Y	N

As can be seen in Figure 2.2 above, there is also a high level of consensus about the components of standards. All the examples contain the following:
- Reference Number – often indicating the place of the standard within a broader framework of standards
- Title – a succinct summary of the outcome to be achieve by those carrying out the function

- Descriptor/Description/Purpose – a brief description of what the standard is about and whom it is for
- Performance Criteria/Assessment Criteria/Evidence Requirements – the key behaviours that can be observed when a worker is carrying out the function competently, which can be used for assessment purposes.

The Australian, New Zealand and South African standards break the function down into a number of *Elements, Outcomes or Specific Outcomes* which act as sub-titles, describing sub-functions of the main function defined by the tile of the standard. All the standards, apart from the New Zealand example, define the *Knowledge and Skills* (in the UK example referred to as "Understanding how to") required for competent performance. All the examples, except that from the UK, have a section called *Range, Scope or Explanatory Notes*, which help to define the context and the range of variables workers need to be able to cope with. Some standards, such as the Australian, New Zealand and South African examples are clearly written for qualifications purposes and also contain Assessment Guidance.

Whilst it is clear that those responsible for compiling standards in each country have referred to cases found elsewhere (for instance, many expressions in the New Zealand and South African examples are identical), there is very little evidence in the hospitality or justice and security sector of collaborative efforts to develop skills standards for use across national borders. By contrast, there are a number of transnational initiatives seeking to define IT functions, knowledge and skills.

SKILLS FRAMEWORK FOR THE INFORMATION AGE

In 2003, the London-based SFIA Foundation established the Skills Framework for the Information Age (SFIA) as a system for IT Professionals to match the skills of the workforce to the requirements of the business. Covering the whole of the IT domain, this two-dimensional skills framework defines areas of work on one axis and levels of responsibility on the other. Illustrative of this approach is the *service desk and incident management* (area of work) level 3 (level of responsibility), defined as: *Receives and handles requests for support following agreed procedures. Responds to* requests *for support by providing information to enable incident resolution and promptly allocates unresolved calls as appropriate. Maintains records and advises relevant persons of actions taken.* Used widely throughout the English-speaking world, the SFIA framework provides a high-level overview of the functions to be carried out, without specifying detailed criteria for assessing performance or the knowledge and skills required.

THE EUROPEAN E-COMPETENCE FRAMEWORK

Developed by a large number of European ICT and HR experts in the context of the CEN (European Committee for Standardization) Workshop on ICT Skills, the European e-Competence Framework (e-CF) is a reference framework of ICT competences that can be used and understood by ICT user and supply companies, ICT practitioners, managers and HR departments, the public sector, educational and social partners across Europe.

THE E-CF IS STRUCTURED IN 4 DIMENSIONS:

Dimension 1: 5 e-Competence areas, derived from the ICT business processes PLAN – BUILD – RUN – ENABLE – MANAGE

Dimension 2: A set of reference e-Competences for each area, with a generic description for each competence. 32 competences identified in total provide the European generic reference definitions of the e-CF 2.3

Dimension 3: Proficiency levels of each e-Competence provide European reference level specifications on e-Competence levels e-1 to e-5, which are related to the EQF levels 3 to 8

Dimension 4: Samples of knowledge and skills relate to e-Competences in dimension 2. They are provided to add value and context and are not intended to be exhaustive.

FIGURE 2.3 USER SUPPORT IN THE E-CF

DIMENSION 1 e-Competence area	C. RUN				

DIMENSION 2	C.1. USER SUPPORT				
e-Competences: title & generic description	Responds to user requesta and issues; records relevant information. Resolves or escalates incidents and optimises system performance. Monitors solution outcome and resultant customer satisfaction.				

DIMENSION 3	LEVEL 1	LEVEL 2	LEVEL 3	LEVEL 4	LEVEL 5
e-Competences: proficiency levels (on e-CF levels e-1 to e-5, related to EQF levels 3 to 8)	Routinely interacts with users, applies ICT-product, basic knowledge and skill to respond to user requests. Solves simple incidents, following prescribed procedures.	Systematically interprets user problems identifying the solutions and possible side effects. Uses experience to identify user problems and interrogates database for potential solutions. Escalates complex or unresolved incidents to sebior experts. Records and tracks user support procedures from outset to conclusion.	Manages the support process and is accountable for ensuring that agreed service levels are met. Plans resource allocation to ensure that the support is available with respect to the defined service level. Acts creatively, and seeks opportunities for continuous service improvement by analysing root causes. Manages the budget of the support function.	-	-

DIMENSION 4					
Knowledge examples	*Knows / Aware of / Familiar with:* **K1** relevant ICT user applications **K2** database structures and content organisation **K3** corporate escalation procedures **K4** software distribution methods and procedures for fix application and file transmission methodologies applicable to software fixes **K5** sources of information for potential solutions				
Skills examples	*Able to:* **S1** effectively interrogate users to establish symptoms **S2** analyse symptoms to identify broad area of user error or technical failure **S3** deploy support tools to systematically trace source of error or technical failure **S4** clearly communicate with end users and provide instructions on how to progress issues **S5** record and code issues to support growth and integrity of online tools				

The example in Figure 2.3 shows that Level 2 in the competence User Support within the business process *Run* in the e-CF, addresses a similar function to those covered by the 5 examples of National Occupational Standards (NOS) and by *Service Desk and Incident Management Level 3* in the SFIA. By contrast to the NOS, however, the e-CF does not provide detailed performance criteria and only provides examples, rather than an exhaustive list, of the knowledge and skills required.

INFORMATION TECHNOLOGY INFRASTRUCTURE LIBRARY (ITIL®)

On 26 April 2013, the UK Government announced a joint venture with Capita plc. to market the Civil Service-developed 'best management practice' portfolio of professional standards, including PRINCE2® project management and ITIL® IT services standards, both of which are widely used throughout the English-speaking world.

With a history dating back to the Central Computer and Telecommunications Agency in the 1980s, the 2011 version of the ITIL standards cover the whole of the IT Services domain in 5 volumes: Service Strategy, Service Design, Service Transition, Service Operation and Continual Service Improvement. Whilst the focus of these publications is to provide detailed best practice guidance for how organisations should manage IT services, they also describe the specific roles, functions, knowledge and skills required of individuals, including the Service Desk role.

The scope of ITIL is limited to IT Services Management (it does not cover software development, hardware design or the range of IT enabled services), but, embedded within its broader coverage of organisational requirements for IT services management, it also contains detailed specifications of the functions, knowledge and skills required by workers in this domain. Since ITIL is already established internationally and will be commercially promoted in the future, it has the potential to develop into a global currency for IT services management skills.

EUROPEAN COMPUTER DRIVING LICENCE (ECDL)

For IT users, the European Computer Driving Licence/ International Computer Driving Licence (ECDL/ICDL) has already established itself as an international currency, with certification programmes delivered to over 11 million people in 41 languages across 148 countries through a network of over 24,000 test centres.

EUROPEAN QUALIFICATIONS FRAMEWORK FOR LIFELONG LEARNING (EQF)

In parallel with the establishment of national and transnational standards and qualifications, in recent years we are seeing the development of "exchange-rate mechanisms" to enable qualifications, which are often based on national occupational standards, to be recognised across national borders.

One of the most fully developed of these mechanisms is the European Qualifications Framework for Lifelong Learning (EQF). The EQF is described as "a translation device making qualifications more readable" which helps "learners and workers wishing to move between countries or change jobs or move between educational institutions at home." It links national qualifications frameworks, rather than replacing them.

The EQF describes 8 levels of qualifications in terms of learning outcomes in three domains: knowledge, skills and competence (similar to the main components of standards). On a voluntary basis, qualifications authorities in each European country match the levels in their own national qualifications framework to the EQF. Thus, a qualification awarded at a level in one country's framework that has been matched to level 5 in the EQF would be equivalent to qualifications covering the same subject matter in all other countries which have been matched to EQF level 5.

HOW ARE SKILLS CURRENCIES USED?

In many countries, such as Australia, New Zealand and South Africa, the primary use of standards is to underpin their Technical and Vocational Education and Training (TVET) systems by providing benchmarks for education, training and qualifications. Standards are written in such a way that they can be used to assess candidates' knowledge, skills and on-the-job performance.

Standards cover functions that form part of a worker's job role; individual standards can be grouped together to form a qualification that reflects a complete job role. In the emerging Indian system, Qualifications Packs (QPs) are being developed containing all the standards relating to a job role, together with assessment guidance. The QP for an IT Service Helpdesk Attendant, for example, contains the following standards:

- SSC/N 0101 Deal remotely with basic IT service requests/incidents
- 9001 Manage your work to meet requirements
- 9002 Work effectively with colleagues
- 9003 Maintain a healthy, safe and secure working environment
- 9004 Provide data/information in standard formats
- 9005 Develop your knowledge, skills and competence.

Because the standards are unitised, each standard is associated with a separate function; QPs can be assembled comprising specialist standards (e.g. SSC/N 0101 *Deal remotely with basic IT service requests/incidents*) and generic standards (e.g. 9001-5), which are common to many roles. This unitisation supports the transferability of skills, the mobility of labour and the flexibility of the workforce; workers take their already-recognised, transferable skills with them to new jobs where they only need to develop their knowledge, skills and competence in the new specialist functions.

Standards can be used as a wider human resource management tool – see figure 2.4.

FIGURE 2.4 USING STANDARDS FOR HR MANAGEMENT AND DEVELOPMENT

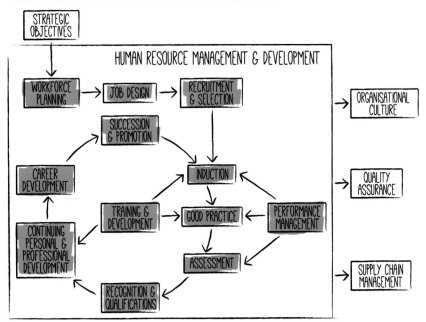

As shown in figure 2.4 above, standards can be used to help plan the workforce cycle needed to deliver an organisation's strategic objectives. Benchmarks are developed by analysing all the functions that need to be carried out to achieve the key purpose of the sector, and by identifying the standards of performance required. People's jobs can therefore be designed and job descriptions created, taking account of both strategic objectives and individual competences. Standards also list the knowledge and skills that workers need, so they provide a good basis for developing person specifications that can be used for assessing and selecting candidates during recruitment or promotion.

Standards can then be used throughout the human resource management and development cycle to:

- identify what people new to posts need to learn and what skills they need to develop during their *induction* period
- provide workers with guidance on what is expected of them and a model of *good practice* when they are carrying out unfamiliar activities
- develop objectives with individual workers and teams and support them in improving their *performance* and achieving their objectives
- *assess* whether workers are performing to the required standards, and if not where the problems may lie
- identify *learning* needs, design training and development activities and evaluate the impact of training and development on the individual worker's knowledge and skills, their performance and the achievement of strategic objectives
- recognise competent performance through *feedback, reward* and qualifications
- provide a clear framework so that individuals can plan, manage and evaluate their own *continuing personal and professional development*
- help individuals *understand what is involved in new posts* they might like to apply for, what competences they could bring to these posts, and what new knowledge and skills they would need to develop
- *prepare individuals to take over from others* when they leave or retire, and select the right individuals for the jobs.

Using standards impacts on organisational culture, as all employees work to a model of good practice and take personal responsibility for delivering a quality service in line with their organisation's quality framework. They also provide a common language for different organisations in the supply chain to communicate with each other, negotiate and agree the standards expected, support each others' work and hold each other to account.

Standards (and related qualifications, through mechanisms like the EQF) are becoming used more widely by organisations to assess the calibre of applicants they are recruiting from overseas and also by governments to inform decisions on the eligibility of immigrants for work permits. Both employers accessing international labour markets and governments wishing to make equitable immigration decisions would benefit from a single transnational benchmark of skills.

WHO WOULD BENEFIT FROM A COMMON SKILLS CURRENCY?

A common skills currency would offer specific benefits to each of the various stakeholder groups involved: learners, jobseekers, employees, employers, customers, governments and society as a whole.

Employers would be able to recruit from the global, rather than just the local labour pool. The common currency would allow them to make transparent comparisons between the credentials of candidates from various parts of the world and select the best candidates for the job. This is especially important where the local talent pool is unable to furnish suitably skilled personnel.

Employers would also be able to compare their own conventions with international benchmarks and improve their practices, quality, effectiveness and productivity as a result. At the same time, they could identify those aspects of jobs that are unique to their organisation or jurisdiction and ensure new recruits receive the necessary induction training to ensure they become productive as soon as possible.

Employees would understand the standards of performance expected of someone in their role and be able to take the initiative to ensure they have the necessary knowledge and skills to perform to world-class standards. They would also be in a position to understand the requirements of other job roles, both in their own and other organisations, and take charge of their own career development, acquiring the new knowledge and skills needed for their next career move.

Jobseekers would be clear about the requirements of job vacancies and whether they possess the necessary knowledge and skills to meet these requirements. Jobseekers with credentials expressed in the common currency would be able to demonstrate to employers anywhere in the world that their profiles meet the person specifications, thus opening up a much wider range of job opportunities for them.

Learners, both pre-employment and in employment, would be clear about what knowledge and skills they need to acquire in order to perform to world-class standards in their chosen occupation. They would be able to select courses and learning materials that have been designed specifically to cover the required curriculum. Having decided on their career, their choice would not be what to learn (that would be defined by the common currency) but *how* they wish to learn it and *how* much they can afford to pay.

Customers would benefit from a guarantee of world-class products and services from organisations using the common currency. When procuring supplies or commissioning services from various companies throughout the world, business customers would be able to check whether vendors are working to the common benchmarks. If they are, they can be assured of the quality of delivery and, if necessary, use the common benchmarks as tools to manage and improve vendor performance. For example, a garment factory in South East Asia working to a overseas high street retailer will develop its organisational job roles according to the common benchmarks which will, in turn, enable any shortfalls in skills and competencies to be easily identified and addressed through tailored training plans. These common benchmarks might include the control environment in which the garment workers operate. The common skills currency would provide education and training providers with a ready-made curriculum to ensure their courses and learning materials cover the knowledge and skills employers need their staff to possess.

Compliance with the common currency would be a guarantee for learners and employers that courses and learning materials are fit-for-purpose and quality-marked as such – a significant marketing benefit. This would also mean that courses and learning materials are not only relevant to a narrow local market but also rendered marketable throughout the world. Education and learning opportunities could be made available in places where they are not currently viable, development costs could be amortised over a much larger learner population and providers would be able to invest significantly to increase the efficacy and accessibility of their offerings.

The benefits to governments are significant. The common skills currency would go a long way to addressing problems in labour/skills demand and supply. For nations with a shortage of appropriately skilled labour, a factor that may be hampering economic growth or social development, the common currency would provide access to the global labour pool. For other nations with a labour surplus, it would provide a means of either exporting labour and repatriating wages, or offering local outsourced services to foreign companies, or encouraging foreign investment with the guarantee of a readily available labour force trained to international standards.

The common skills currency would also facilitate the development and implementation of a fair, rational and transparent immigration policy. The skills in short supply locally could be identified by employers and defined in terms of the international benchmarks. Migrant jobseekers with necessary credentials could be admitted quickly in line with immigration policy and without additional bureaucratic processes. This would both reduce the administrative burden on employers and immigration departments and accelerate economic development.

Those nations without structured systems of occupational standards and qualifications frameworks would be able to use the international benchmarks as a proxy, perhaps adding elements to reflect local practices and regulations, and thus develop a world-class vocational education and training system at a fraction of the cost. The economic benefits are apparent as those countries that guarantee work to international standards are more attractive destinations both for foreign investment and for tourism. Even those countries with their own well-developed systems could seize opportunities to collaborate transnationally in developing standards and qualifications for new occupations or in domains where no frameworks currently exist.

Lastly, society as a whole can benefit from the TnSS system, as it creates reduced costs and reliable methods of training in detection and prevention of transnational crime. Crime is an international phenomenon and problems such as organised crime, drug trafficking and cybercrime cannot be tackled by one jurisdiction in isolation. Governments need to work collaboratively to develop common standards to support the prevention and detection of crimes that transcend national borders, the care of victims, and the arrest, prosecution and detention of perpetrators. The benefits will be reductions in the cost of crime and a safer and more secure environment.

A safer and more secure environment is a benefit that the whole of society will enjoy. However, society would also benefit from a greater and more varied range of employment opportunities, improved quality of products and services, reduced costs deriving from economies of scale and increased wealth as a result of a freer labour and skills market. The initial investment in a common skills currency would be marginal for such a significant return.

CHAPTER THREE
TRANSNATIONAL SKILLS STANDARDS

STREET CLEANER
Santiago

In the previous chapter we outlined the rationale for a new skills currency: the key drivers, uses and benefits to the range of stakeholders. In this chapter we consider what the new coinage might look like. What are the main operating principles that might underpin TnSS?

FUNCTIONS NOT JOBS

The first principle is that TnSS describe functions – activities or tasks that workers carry out – rather than complete job roles. Many work functions – such as "serve food", "check passports", "develop software code" – are similar wherever in the world they are carried out. By contrast, the way jobs are constructed differs significantly according to the context.

The job of a waiter in a Michelin starred restaurant may be restricted to taking customers' orders, serving food and checking from time to time on their level of satisfaction. In a small family restaurant, the owner may greet and seat customers, take and serve both food and drink orders, prepare the bill, process payment and carry out general public relations duties. Typically, the smaller the enterprise the wider the range of functions found in any individual's job role. A border officer at an international airport may be required to validate the entry entitlement of thousands of passengers every day. At a small road crossing, checking passports may be just one of a wider range of immigration and customs duties the border guard has to carry out.

In order that TnSS can succeed within this range of different contexts, it is important that the unit of currency is the function, which is universally understood, rather than a job or occupation that may be constructed differently in response to the national, organisational or local context.

OUTCOMES NOT PROCESSES

A second principle of the new currency is its focus on outcomes – the results of work – rather than the processes needed to achieve them. The outcomes that workers are required to deliver – "serve food to restaurant tables as ordered by customers", "validate the entitlement of travelers to enter the country", "produce software code to technical specifications" – will be broadly similar anywhere in the world, but the processes and procedures that must be followed will vary according to national, organisational or local contexts.

TnSS should therefore focus attention on the outcomes required – is the food served as the customers order it?, are the travelers entitled to enter the country?, does the software code meet the specifications? – rather than attempting to describe the process in detail.

UNIVERSALLY-APPLICABLE AND CONTEXT SPECIFIC

To be effective, TnSS must provide a simple universally applicable framework to which individual jurisdictions can add context-specific components. TnSS need to be able to work in any country or organisation where the functions they describe are carried out. They cannot, therefore, refer to national legislation, regulations, administrative structures or procedures, nor can they be conditioned by particular technologies, societal norms or organisational requirements. The simplest framework for a Transnational Skills Standard on which it would be possible to achieve international consensus would comprise of three components:

- the outcome workers are expected to achieve (this would be the *title* of the TnSS)
- a description of the performance or behaviors expected of workers in achieving this outcome (these could be called *performance criteria* or *behavioral indicators*)
- a specification of what workers need to know and be able to do in order to achieve the outcome (the *knowledge* and *abilities* required to achieve the outcome).

To this basic framework, individual jurisdictions could then add their own context-specific requirements, such as national or local laws and regulations or organisational-specific policies and procedures. The distinction would, therefore, be clear between the agreed Transnational Skills Standard and the additional requirements employees must meet in order to work in a particular jurisdiction or organisational context.

CONSENSUS

TnSS will only attain international recognition if they are derived through a process that engages with all relevant stakeholder groups from the different countries involved and ensures their contributions are included and concerns addressed. The key stakeholder groups that need to be consulted include:

- employers – subject matter experts within employing organisations have a key role in defining the outcomes of work and the standards of performance they expect from workers
- workers – as the prime agents, workers can make valuable contributions to the definition of standards and they need to agree that the outcomes and performance required of them are achievable
- education and training providers – providers can help define the knowledge and skills required for competent performance and ensure these are included in relevant curricula
- human resource management and development specialists – HR specialists need to consider how to help workers develop their knowledge, skills and competences in line with the TnSS and how the TnSS interface with HR processes and systems
- qualifications providers – organisations that award certificates and qualifications can help to ensure TnSS contribute to transnational recognition of competence and mobility of labour
- standards organisations – sectoral, national and international organisations responsible for setting, maintaining and assuring work-related standards may have benchmarks which can be levered to facilitate the development of TnSS
- legislators, regulators and policy-makers – representatives and officials need to consider the implications and opportunities of TnSS, particularly in the areas of industry/professional regulation, labour market and immigration policy and broader economic, social and foreign policy
- researchers and academics – academia and research organisations will have valuable information to contribute to the development of TnSS and may play an important role in their evaluation.

Many of these stakeholder groups will be accessed through their representative organisations, such as industry bodies, sector councils or trades unions. It is not necessary that all stakeholders agree on every detail of the TnSS. It is, however, important that consensus is reached that TnSS provide an acceptable definition of the performance, knowledge and abilities required to achieve defined outcomes at work.

EXISTING STANDARDS

As seen in Chapter 2, there are many examples of national standards defining the performance, knowledge and abilities required of workers. There are fewer international benchmarks, although those that do exist – such as Skills for the Information Age, European e-Competence Framework, Information Technology Infrastructure Library and European Computer Driving Licence –can be leveraged to inform the development of TnSS. Reference should be made to existing standards and benchmarks to clarify how, and to what extent, these relate to TnSS.

DYNAMIC

The three sectors considered in depth in Chapter 2 – hospitality, IT and justice and security – are all subject to rapid change and innovation. The Internet, combined with new service models, has permitted travelers to become far more directly engaged in identifying, designing and booking their travel arrangements. Cybercrime is a phenomenon borne out in the Internet with increasingly ingenious criminals requiring ever-more sophisticated responses and skills from law-enforcement agencies. New technologies create completely new skills demands, whilst at the same time eliminating the need for other skills, and, in some cases, for entire job roles.

TnSS will need to respond rapidly to the changing environment; they cannot be agreed upon and then left to atrophy. There will need to be a continuous process to ensure new TnSS are developed to address emerging needs, obsolete functions are deleted, and amendments made promptly in response to significant changes in the performance, knowledge and skills demands placed on workers.

METHODOLOGY FOR DEVELOPING TRANSNATIONAL SKILLS STANDARDS

What methodology, or mix of methodologies, might be deployed to ensure TnSS comply with these principles?

Whatever methodologies are used, they must enable the following:

- **Precise definition of the domain or area of work to be covered by the TnSS.**
  Food and Beverage Service, Software Product Development or *Cybercrime* could be potential domains. Such broad titles can, however, be open to interpretation, particularly about their scope (what is to be covered and what is not to be covered by the TnSS).

- **Identification of the stakeholders in the TnSS and how they should be involved.**
  Stakeholders will include workers in all the occupations and jobs covered in the domain, organisations who employ these workers, plus all the other stakeholders who can either contribute knowledge and expertise to the development of the TnSS or benefit from using the TnSS for education, training, HR management, partnership, quality assurance, regulatory or political purposes.

- **Identification of existing standards that are relevant to the domain.**
  These can be utilised to save time and resources in the development of TnSS.

- **Specification of all the functions that have to be carried out in the domain.**
  These will become the titles of the TnSS.

- **Definition of competent performance for each function.**
  What does competent performance look like when workers are carrying out each function?

- **Definition of knowledge and abilities for each function.**
  What do workers need to know and what do they need to be able to do in order to attain the outcomes of each function?

No single methodology will be able to address all these requirements. However, there is a choice of tried-and-tested methodologies that can be deployed. *Occupational Mapping*, for example, can be employed to define clearly the domain to be covered and provide valuable information regarding the occupations and jobs affected, the employers involved and current systems for initial education and continuing professional development. *Stakeholder Analysis* is a familiar methodology to identify all the stakeholders, their interests and how and when they need to be engaged in the development, implementation and evaluation of TnSS. Internet and telephone research amongst standards-setting organisations should be sufficient to identify relevant suites of standards that can be utilised in the development of TnSS. *Functional Analysis* is an effective tool to identify both current and future functions relevant to the domain. Functional Analysis starts with the key purpose of the domain (what everyone working in the domain is striving to achieve) and, through a repetitive process of disaggregation, identifies all the functions that individual workers need to carry out in order to achieve the key purpose.

Once the functions have been defined and agreed by the stakeholders, there are a number of methodologies and individual techniques that can be deployed to define competent performance in each function, together with the knowledge and abilities required, including:
- Competency Analysis Profiling
- Critical Incident Technique
- DACUM (Developing a Curriculum)
- Delphi Technique
- Diary Method
- Fleishman Job Analysis
- National Occupational Standards (NOS) Development
- Observation
- Task Analysis
- Work Process Analysis
- Workshops with Subject Matter Experts (SMEs).

It is likely that a hybrid methodology will need to be created to facilitate the development of suites of TnSS. The TnSS development methodology will first need to engage with SMEs (expert workers, their supervisors and educators/trainers) representing the various countries and different types and sizes of employing organisations involved, and then facilitate processes to help the SMEs *articulate what competent performance should look like* when carrying out each function, *specify the knowledge and abilities required* for competent performance in each function and arrive at consensus on the performance, knowledge and skills requirements for each function.

STRUCTURE OF TRANSNATIONAL SKILLS STANDARDS

There are currently no TnSS developed according to the mix of methodologies proposed. However, in order to understand what TnSS might look like we have leveraged available national standards from around the world to create a prototype based on the IT helpdesk example considered in Chapter 2.

IT helpdesk workers can be sitting anywhere in the world where there is a broadband connection as long as they have the necessary technical know-how and can communicate in a common language with the customer. The IT helpdesk is a classic candidate for outsourcing to remote locations with workforces possessing high education levels, good language skills and low salary expectations.

For this TnSS prototype, we have used a structure involving the following components:

- Reference Number – a unique reference number, indicating the suite of TnSS (e.g. using the prefix 'IT' for Information Technology) and the position of the standard within that suite: IT001
- Title – the function described in terms of the outcome the worker must achieve
- Description – a concise summary which clearly indicates what the standard is about and who it is for (the description may also indicate what is outside the designation of the standard)

- Scope – listings of the range of variables that have a critical impact on the quality of performance required
- Performance Requirements – behaviors workers are expected to display when carrying out the function
- Knowledge Requirements – specifications of what workers need to know and understand to perform competently
- Ability Requirements – specifications of what workers need to be able to do to perform competently
- Context Requirements – blank space for the addition of the specific requirements of individual jurisdictions or organisations.

TNSS PROTOTYPE FROM THE IT SECTOR

REFERENCE NUMBER	IT001
TITLE	**Deal remotely with basic IT service requests/incidents**
DESCRIPTION	This standard is about dealing with basic service requests and incidents at the IT helpdesk and referring more complex problems to technicians or subject matter experts for resolution.
PERFORMANCE REQUIREMENTS	*To perform competently, you must*: • confirm to **customers** that you have received the **service requests/incidents** • express your concern for any difficulties caused and your commitment to resolving them • obtain sufficient information from **customers** to understand the nature of the **problems** and perform initial diagnosis • record and categorise **service requests/incidents** accurately using your organisation's systems • access your organisation's knowledge base and suppliers' reference sources, where required, to find solutions to **problems** • support **customers** remotely to test potential solutions • prioritise **service requests/incidents** according to organisational guidelines • provide **customers** with a justifiable estimate of resolution time, where an immediate solution cannot be found • refer problems to **appropriate people**, when the **problems** cannot be resolved at the helpdesk • obtain advice and guidance from **appropriate people** where **problems** are outside your area of competence • monitor **problems** to keep customers informed about progress and any delays in resolving **problems** • obtain confirmation from **customers** that **problems** have been resolved to their satisfaction

PERFORMANCE REQUIREMENTS (CONTINUED)	• record the resolution of **problems** accurately using your organisation's systems • comply with relevant standards, policies, procedures, guidelines and service level agreements (SLAs) when dealing with basic IT service requests/incidents
SCOPE	*To perform competently, you must be able to handle the following variables:* **Customers:** • internal • external **Service requests/incidents** reported via: • voice call • e-mail • internet **Problems** about: • networking/connectivity • operating system/software • installation/configuration • computer hardware • account maintenance/access rights • voice/telephone • video call **Appropriate people:** • colleagues at the IT helpdesk • subject matter experts in your organisation • subject matter experts outside your organisation • your supervisor

KNOWLEDGE REQUIREMENTS	*To perform competently, you need to know and understand*: • relevant standards, policies, procedures, guidelines and SLAs for dealing with basic IT service requests/incidents • the range of methods and techniques to provide customer service • your organisation's systems for dealing with basic IT service requests/incidents, and how to use them • the range of common problems at the helpdesk and how to resolve them • how to access your organisation's knowledge base • suppliers' reference sources and how to access them • techniques used to test potential solutions remotely with customers • limits of your role and responsibilities in relation to IT service requests/incidents • whom to refer problems to when they cannot be resolved at the IT helpdesk • the importance of keeping customers informed about timescales, progress and resolution of service requests/incidents • the importance of obtaining confirmation from customers that problems have been resolved to their satisfaction

ABILITY REQUIREMENTS	*To perform competently, you must be able to*: • communicate with customers in writing in a common language • listen carefully to customers • communicate with customers orally in a common language • ask for clarification and advice from others • follow standards, policies, procedures, guidelines and SLAs • apply problem-solving approaches to common problems • follow rule-based decision-making processes • make decisions on a suitable course of action or response • plan and organise your work to achieve targets and deadlines • build and maintain positive and effective relationships with customers • check your work is complete and free from errors • deliver consistent and reliable service to customers • pass on relevant information to others • work independently and collaboratively within a team environment • use information technology effectively to input and extract data accurately • keep up to date with changes in your role • keep up to date with changes in your field of expertise
CONTEXT REQUIREMENTS	*To perform competently in your particular context, you must be able to*: (requirements for individual jurisdictions / organisations to be added locally)

This TnSS prototype has been developed by drawing on national standards from around the world and leveraging the emerging international frameworks identified in our research. Making best use of existing standards is one of the principles established at the beginning of the chapter. This prototype also complies with three further principles. It describes a particular function: *Deal remotely with basic IT service requests/incidents*, rather than the whole job role of the Helpdesk Worker, which is likely to involve a range of other functions, depending on how the organisation designs the job. It focuses on the outcome – dealing with the IT problem – rather than the detailed processes and procedures involved, which again will vary from one organisation to another. It is universally applicable, relevant to any IT helpdesk function anywhere in the world, whilst allowing, in the final section, space for adding any requirements relating to the particular context.

To comply fully with the principles, what remains to be done is to achieve consensus on the TnSS prototype with all the relevant stakeholder groups and ensure that the standard responds dynamically to changes in practice, technology, regulation and legislation over time. How this might be achieved is described in the next chapter.

CHAPTER FOUR

MINTING THE NEW CURRENCY

SOUND ENGINEER,
London

Minting the new skills currency to aid better mobility and build better lives is an urgent task. Global unemployment now stands at nearly 200 million, and a further 39 million have dropped out of the labour market since the outbreak of the global financial crisis in 2008 because of the difficulty in finding a job to match their skillset. According to the International Labour Organization, the *length and depth of the labour market crisis is worsening labour market mismatch, contributing to extended spells of unemployment. New jobs that become available often require competences that the unemployed do not possess. Such skill and occupational mismatches will make the labour market react more slowly to any acceleration in activity over the medium run, unless supporting policies to re-skill and activate current jobseekers are enhanced.*[22]

In the United States – a G7 country – the debate is intensifying over the planned overhaul of the country's prosaic immigration system. While a foreign entrepreneur with a great idea or a new invention can start a business with a H1B Visa, they cannot work for the company that they created. Anomalies like this, as well as the lack of universally recognised skills or competency-based decision-making criteria for granting visas, make it difficult for national governments to tap into the potential high-growth generating, highly-skilled migrant labour market. There's no denying that immigration will remain a political minefield, but the economic costs of inaction may end up seriously inhibiting the next wave of globalisation and inclusive growth.

The OECD agrees that skills mismatch is one of the most significant challenges faced by economies today, with the unavailability of required skills providing a brake on economic growth.[23] At the individual level, over-skilled workers are capable of handling more complex tasks and their skills are under-utilised, often resulting in poor job satisfaction and high staff turnover. Under-skilling, on the other hand, can affect productivity and slow the rate at which more efficient technologies and approaches to work can be adopted. The OECD encourages policies that both improve the supply of skills which employers require and, simultaneously support managers, particularly in small and medium enterprises to make the best use of the skills available to them.

India is the second most populous country with more than 1.2 billion citizens, almost as many as North America and Europe combined. Recognising that skills and knowledge are the driving forces of economic growth and social development for any country, the National Skills Development Policy[24] seeks to equip 500 million Indians with the skills needed to help them secure "decent work" in a global marketplace. In contrast to the ageing West and a declining population in Russia, India's productive capacity is increasing and will reach 800 million by 2015, even more than China's 600 million. The Indian Ministry of Labour estimates that, by 2020, the world may have a shortage of 47 million workers but India will have a surplus of 56 million people who will need to be equipped with the skills to compete globally and to cash in on this potential "demographic dividend".

BRICS countries like India and its National Skills Development Corporation has charged a number of organisations representing employers in strategic economic sectors, such as agriculture, financial services, construction, electronics, healthcare, IT-ITeS, logistics, media and entertainment and telecoms, with developing the skills required. These *Sector Skills Councils* are currently defining *National Occupational Standards* – specifications of standards of performance, knowledge and skills required when carrying out work activities – which can then be used by schools, colleges and universities to develop relevant curricula and form the basis of qualifications which can be benchmarked internationally. There is nothing new about NOS, but India is trying to ensure their much wider application and use. It will be another 2-3 years before we know whether this experiment has been successful.

Gazelle countries like Pakistan and Bangladesh are embarked on similar strategies of Technical and Vocational Education and Training (TVET) reform, as are Egypt and the MENA countries. Whilst there may be subtle differences in individual countries' motivations and methodologies, our *Four Worlds of Human Capital model*, discussed in Chapter 1, shows that there is a common driver amongst this group of countries to secure the economic prosperity and social stability that result from a better match of skills supply to demand. Paradoxically, although maximum use is being made of existing benchmarks, particularly those developed in North America, Europe and

Australasia over the past 30 years, each country is minting its own skills currency rather than collaborating on a common currency that can be spent throughout the world. Apart from the costs involved in this piecemeal development, these individual currencies mean that employers cannot enjoy the benefits of a single currency when recruiting from abroad, outsourcing processes to a foreign country or planning to invest in a new region.

Neither will job-seekers be able to get full value for their national credentials when seeking positions overseas. Both the OECD[25] and the International Organization for Migration (IOM)[26] recognise that there is under-utilisation of the human capital of immigrants and insufficient recognition of their qualifications, even though host countries are actively seeking skilled labour. The IOM's report, *Recognition of the Qualifications and Competences of Migrants*, highlights the complexity of European, Canadian and Australian immigration systems as a key barrier to importing the skills these ageing populations need. It also points out that not only formal qualifications, but also informal and non-formal learning need to be recognised in assessing immigrants' competences in order to facilitate "job mobility and the matching between migrants' skills and labour market needs, with a view to addressing skill gaps."

DEVELOPING AND MAINTAINING TRANSNATIONAL SKILLS STANDARDS

The OECD claims that *skills have become the global currency of the 21st century.* Certainly, skills – people's practical and professional capabilities to achieve results – are precious resources that need to be continuously developed and effectively utilised to ensure future prosperity. To date, however, these skills have been expressed in local currencies – national standards and qualifications – with complex exchange-rate mechanisms, inequitable rates of exchange and high commissions payable in order to redeem them in other jurisdictions. TnSS offer a single currency so that those skills that are fungible or tradable can command equal value anywhere in the world, providing the labour market in question is operating in an open system of exchange.

Our detailed sector research has identified a need for a common skills currency, that is universally recognisable and that the denomination of units, acting as a store of 'value', is easily understood. This is perhaps best illustrated by the adoption, in antiquity, of Arabic mathematics as the basis for a universally recognised and accepted numeric system. The need for a common understanding of the descriptors of TnSS will also need to be considered, and as such, the need for a common language describing the knowledge, functions, levels of competence and proficiency may well emerge.

The question therefore on the lips of employers, individuals, multi-national bodies and national governments is, 'How will this work?'

PRINCIPLE 1: DEMAND-LED

It is recognised that TnSS will need to build a demand-driven dynamic that can be developed and maintained through collaboration of the key stakeholders, whether these be nations; cross-national groups such as the European Union; international organisations with interests in labour market development or expertise in the sectors involved; or employers and employer/employee led organisations. At national level this equates to the government departments or agencies responsible for skills development, the social partners representing employers and workers, and leading research, academic and professional institutions in the relevant sectors. These national stakeholders will in turn need to have the commitment to and participation in both national dialogue and development of TnSS. INSSO therefore proposes an infrastructure to engage with all the stakeholders and other critical partners such as the OECD, UNESCO, ILO, World Bank and relevant international workforce development and professional groups. Only at that level of engagement will the drive emerge to create the systemic process for developing, recognising and accrediting TnSS. This infrastructure is outlined below in Principles 3 and 4.

It is fair to say that although TnSS have all the signs of being the most effective solution, it was never going to be a cheap way to tackle the global talent gap. The common languages and rule governing free trade were not solved overnight, so TnSS should not be presented as some kind of magic bullet solution to global imbalances in labour supply and demand.

To take TnSS to the next level, INSSO will be working with partners to identify *more information*, including existing standards, benchmarks or good practice guidelines which can be used as the basis for TnSS and details about any national laws or regulations which may limit the application of TnSS.

PRINCIPLE 2: OPEN-SOURCE ACCESS

The best global currencies allow open access to them but that does not necessarily mean that TnSS will be free. We have identified three funding models that require further discussion. The first option involves a multi-lateral organisation funding the development of TnSS, over 3 years, to enable an open-source public platform for accessing TnSS. In this scenario, TnSS would be available on a royalty-free basis. The second option is more of a hybrid, public-private partnership, where an open source platform is developed offering both 'freemium' and 'premium' services relating to TnSS. In this scenario, access to view the TnSS could remain free, but their use and application – for example as training packages used by vocational institutes – would cost a royalty fee. The third type of model is essentially a private sector led subscription or royalty-based approach where full charging would need to occur in order to recoup the private-sector investment. It is possible in this scenario that TnSS could be priced sensitively so that poorer countries could access them at cost or less. This would include their use within TVET systems and within organisational skills development programmes, qualifications and frameworks. Concomitantly, revenue for the maintenance and development of TnSS could be generated through licensing their use within commercial training packages, qualifications, human resources management systems and other avenues. These revenue streams could contribute to the ongoing management and maintenance of TnSS and ensure that they are kept up-to-date and sustainable over time.

FIGURE 4.1: ACHIEVING TRANSNATIONAL SKILLS STANDARDS

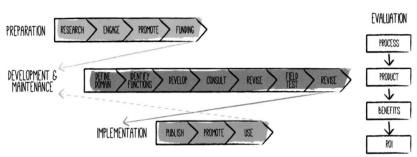

PRINCIPLE 3: DEEPER CONSULTATION

INSSO has recognised that before work can start on developing TnSS, a preparation phase will need to be completed involving: detailed research into all identified sectors, engagement with stakeholders in the different countries, making the business case and ensuring the availability of the resources required. The development phase for the first tranche of sector-based TnSS is likely to last up to 18 months in order to gain consensus on the standards, knowledge and abilities required to perform effectively in all the functions identified. Support will need to be made available for the implementation of TnSS, both promoting and facilitating their use by stakeholders. Each stage of the process, the outcomes, benefits and return on investment (ROI) would need to be carefully evaluated.

Achieving TnSS, even for a single strategic sector, will potentially involve a significant and complex programme of work. It is proposed that a new centre of excellence, to be known as the Occupational Standards Competency and Accreditation (OSCA) centre, manages this programme. INSSO is actively considering how this could best operate, as a spin-off independent entity or an autonomous unit within INSSO. At this stage, we propose to establish OSCA – as a physical and virtual centre, with six main objectives:

1. *Labour market* research to understand and anticipate the skills needs, gaps and mismatches in supply and demand and evaluate policy approaches to address them

2. *Stakeholder engagement* to identify stakeholders in the different sectors, evaluate their interests and implement strategies to ensure their active participation in the development and use of TnSS. This would include the support of the project management of the TnSS development and implementation process within each identified sector, whether led by a sector-based consortia or sector-lead body standards development and maintenance to apply proven and innovative methodologies and techniques in the creation and updating of TnSS that comply with agreed principles and criteria

3. *Consultancy with policy makers and organisations* to facilitate the use of TnSS to develop and make effective use of required skills

4. *Training of professionals* in the methodologies and techniques for developing and applying TnSS

5. *Evaluation* to assure quality and measure the economic and social return on investment from TnSS

6. *Registration, maintenance and review of TnSS and the creation of an e-platform for approval, accreditation, access and application*

We will publish further details about how OSCA will operate, including its physical location, in the coming months.

PRINCIPLE 4: PROVIDE A CLEAR LEGACY FOR COUNTRIES

There is a clear need to ensure that the expertise brought or gained from engagement in the build, design, development and operation of TnSS is available to all of its participating organisations. How TnSS are put to use will determine the competitive advantage to be gained, not their creation or access per se. Further work needs to be done to examine how TnSS could be available as a public good, accessible by all. In the experience of INSSO, both in delivering Occupational Standards to a range of sectors and countries and the development of appropriate sector or industry based skills models, there is a need for all countries to be able to help themselves. While there is a significant foreign consultancy market in skills standards expertise, we do not believe it is a long-term solution for countries or the global economy as a whole. Our OSCA proposal is designed to create an infrastructure of support and expert knowledge transfer, internationally recognised, that can act as a repository of workforce development know-how that will enhance the capacity of a country, sector or organisation, by embedding a legacy of indigenous expertise.

CONCLUSION AND NEXT STEPS

This publication has drawn on research into current processes for skills development and the needs for, and projected benefits of, TnSS in three sectors: IT and IT enabled services, justice and security, tourism and hospitality, each are outlined below. Separate reports on each of these sectors will be published in due course.

It is recognised that there are *de facto* examples of transnational standards already in existence such as those for personal computer users in the European/International Computer Driving Licence. However, given the global nature of the IT industry, the development of further demand-driven common skills standards is recognised as being of significant benefit to organisations, employees, freelancers and job-seekers in the IT services management domain. The Skills Framework for the Information Age (SFIA) is a high-level framework for the whole of the IT sector, the e-Competence Framework offers greater depth at a European level while the ITIL provides a very detailed organisational perspective. These three frameworks could provide the foundations for a quick win in developing consensus on TnSS for IT services management. All the major IT services companies operating in India have recently been engaged in agreeing national occupational standards covering their workers' skills. The IT-ITeS sector skills council in India, NASSCOM, is keen to take a lead role in engaging sister organisations around the world in developing the first IT TnSS.

Research in the justice and security sector focused on three areas which had been flagged up by international agencies, including UNESCO, as potential beneficiaries of TnSS: cybercrime, human trafficking and prisons/corrections. Whilst there are long-standing national standards for prisons/corrections and more recent developments in response to national strategies on cybercrime and human trafficking, there are no examples of international collaboration on standards covering these domains. However, there are a number of cross-national and multi-national agreements and protocols on cybercrime and human trafficking. These, combined with the nascent national standards in these areas, could be levered to produce TnSS covering the prevention, detection, arrest, prosecution and care of victims of these crimes that are clearly transnational in nature and require concerted and consistent transnational responses. The case for TnSS for prisons/corrections is focused on the benefits that a common approach would bring to help ensure the upholding of international agreements on human rights for the treatment of offenders. The UK has more than 20 years' experience in developing skills standards in the justice and security sector and training law-enforcement agencies internationally. The UK sector skills council, Skills for Justice, is well placed to lead the development of TnSS in these critical areas.

In 2003, an ILO study of the tourism industry reported that:
Generally, it is at the vocational, non-academic levels that skills shortages are most apparent. Since many jobs in the [tourism] industry do not require academic qualifications, and also because there is generally a shortage of government and private sector vocational training schemes, in many countries the major hotel groups and travel companies tend to rely on their own in-house training abilities. This does not help the many small businesses in the industry, however, who cannot afford the luxury of in-house trainers. The provision of suitable training programs for SMEs is therefore a matter requiring specific attention.[27]

Ten years later, our research found that TnSS could help address many problems in the tourism sector worldwide, including:

- lack of recognition by stakeholders of the importance of training and human resource development as a key component of the tourism product
- high staff turnover and other resource issues associated with seasonality
- forecasted growth rates that far exceed available labour supply
- capabilities of training and education resources, nationally, regionally and corporately
- labour shortages and skills mismatches throughout the economy

- duplicative and uncoordinated human resource development activity across political boundaries which does not properly utilise scarce resources.

The research concluded that TnSS should be concentrated in the food and beverage services and accommodation industries both because of the significant size of their workforce and because the common skills requirements would provide relative transferability between countries and other sectors. The Canadian Tourism Human Resource Council which carried out this research and already has experience in developing international standards for event management would be one choice to lead the development of TnSS for this sector.

Further research and wide-ranging consultation with stakeholders at national and international level will need to be carried out before a decision can be taken on the exact domain to be covered by the first TnSS. However, other sectors with both a high proportion of fungible/tradable skills and significant economic or social impact – banking and financial services, energy, healthcare and logistics, for example – could well form the next tranche for consideration as sectors in urgent need of agreed international specifications for skills. Particularly if these sectors see that there are a number of key and critical internationally recognised skills standards that are required in order to anticipate demand, as the sectors expand rapidly in order to avoid skills gaps resulting from the introduction of new technology or working practices. This current focus on sector specific skills requirements does not preclude the need to look at cross-cutting skills – such as management and customer service – which are used in all sectors. These are also likely to be early candidates for the development of TnSS since their impact will be widely felt throughout all economic activities.

This paper therefore opens the debate on these issues and outlines a practical way forward once they are resolved. The development of TnSS on a rolling, sector-by-sector basis will be a long-term endeavor, perhaps over 10 years or more. The pioneering sectors will have to wrestle with the inevitable problems of working in uncharted territory in order to lay down a clearer path for other sectors to follow. They will, however, enjoy the benefits earlier. Not all nations or employers will want to be involved in the development of TnSS from the outset; indeed, if they did the programme would become unmanageable. INSSO believes that once those benefits become evident, we can expect to see even the most conservative sectors and nations and those employers most protective of their competitive advantage recognising the value of having clearly agreed international standards that allow the right skills to be available at the right time in the right part of the world and maximise their contribution to industry, sector, national and global prosperity.

AND FINALLY, A PAUSE FOR THOUGHT

In 1989, Sir Tim Berners-Lee drafted a paper proposing a model for improving information management within large and complex projects, which his boss at CERN, Mike Sendell, noted was "vague, but exciting." In April 1993, CERN made Berners-Lee's source code for the WorldWideWeb software available royalty-free. Bill Gates famously commented that the Internet would never catch on. By the end of the year there were 500 web servers and the WWW accounted for just 1% of all Internet traffic. Twenty years on, there are an estimated 630 million websites online. In just 3 days, more information is stored digitally, than was the case in all recorded history up until 2003.

Our proposal for TnSS is, we trust, both purposeful and exciting, if still somewhat "vague." The concept still requires consultation and detailed project planning, but, with the right level of stakeholder engagement, we believe we could realise our vision of 630 million people working to TnSS in 15 years time. On the side of a bus in New Delhi, it says "everyone has ideas but few action them." This paper has sought to take the first step in putting ideas for TnSS into action.

ANNEXES

SCIENTIST,
Moscow

GLOSSARY OF TERMS

THE FOUR WORLDS OF HUMAN CAPITAL	An analytical device which divides the world's economies into four regions according to the societal, economic and cultural context in which skills are developed
G7 NATIONS	USA, Canada, Germany, France, Italy, Japan and the UK – 'Advanced and ageing'
BRICS	Brazil, Russia, India, China and South Africa – 'Assertive and rising'
MENA	(Middle East and North Africa): Egypt, Tunisia, Saudi Arabia, Israel, Lebanon and 18 other states – 'Young and changing'
GAZELLES	Nigeria, Singapore, Vietnam, Philippines, Bangladesh, Afghanistan and Indonesia – 'Developing and jumping'
FUNGIBLE SKILLS	fully exchangeable skills applied in an open system of exchange
TRADABLE SKILLS	skills pertaining to skilled trades which are exchangeable but not fungible
UNIQUE SKILLS	skills that are rarely required or where 'star quality' is necessary, operating in a closed system of exchange
SYSTEMS OF EXCHANGE	the extent to which global labour markets are allowed to move freely i.e. be fully mobile. Open systems of exchange are evident by the lack of specific laws, regulation and immigration policies that prevent the free movement of people, the extent of which lead to more closed systems of exchange

PROJECT TEAM

Jack Matthews, Executive Director and TnSS Project Director, INSSO
Tom Bewick, Director and Chief Economist, INSSO
Trevor Boutall, Principal Consultant Partner, INSSO
Emma Evans, Project Manager, INSSO
Dr. Sandhya Chintala, Executive Director, NASSCOM IT/ITeS Sector Skills Council, India
Philip Mondor, Senior Vice-President, Canadian Tourism Human Resource Council
Jon Parry, Head of Research, Skills for Justice, Sector Skills Council, UK

MEMBERS OF THE INTERNATIONAL ADVISORY PANEL

Jack Matthews, Panel Chair and Project Director, INSSO
Tom Bewick, Director and Chief Economist, INSSO
Trevor Boutall, Principal Consultant Partner, INSSO
Manos Kapterian, Managing Director, Pearson Qualifications International
Alan Woods OBE, Chief Executive, Skills for Justice
Dr. Sandhya Chintala, Executive Director, NASSCOM IT/ITeS Sector Skills Council
Philip Mondor, Senior Vice-President, Canadian Tourism Human Resources Council
Andreas Schleicher, Deputy Director for Education, OECD
Borhène Chakroun, Chief of the TVET Section, UNESCO
Dr. Jee-Peng Tan, Education Advisor, World Bank
Mike Campbell OBE, International Skills Expert, Independent Consultant

RESEARCH METHODOLOGY

Research was undertaken in the hospitality and tourism, justice and security and IT and ITeS sectors to provide data on the market for the most applicable occupational standards on which to base TnSS, and to provide an analysis of the gaps in skills demand where such standards would be most valuable. The key aims of the initial research element of the TnSS project were as follows:

- To identify current use of specific international standards related to a particular industrial sector in relation to their coverage, impact and demand across that sector
- To identify occupations and occupational areas that are most strongly linked to the economic growth and sustainability of that sector
- To identify the key occupational standards that would generate most value and benefit from being recognised on an international basis

The research teams were asked to provide an assessment of a range of research and process questions, including macro-economic data, in relation to the specific sectors that were under investigation. The resulting detailed sector research reports are due to be published soon.

Macro-economic data analysis for Figures 1.1 and 1.2 was provided by CFE Research (www.cfe.org.uk). Sources of the data are listed in the table below:

DATA (ALL 2009)	SOURCE
GDP per capita, PPP (constant 2005 international $)	World Bank, International Comparison Program database.
School enrolment, tertiary (% gross). Gross enrolment ratio. Tertiary (ISCED 5 and 6). Total is the total enrolment in tertiary education (ISCED 5 and 6), regardless of age, expressed as a percentage of the total population of the five-year age group following on from secondary school leaving.	United Nations Educational, Scientific, and Cultural Organization (UNESCO) Institute for Statistics.

Labour force, total	International Labour Organization, using World Bank population estimates.
Median Age of the population (medium variant) (2009 only)	Population Division of the Department of Economic and Social Affairs of the United Nations Secretariat (2009). World Population Prospects: The 2008 Revision. Highlights. New York: United Nations.

ACKNOWLEDGEMENTS

INSSO would like to extend sincere thanks to Pearson for supporting the Transnational Skills Standards project from its inception including the production of this publication and the associated research. Sincere thanks are also extended to all of the contributors including the sector lead bodies Skills for Justice, Canadian Tourism Human Resource Council (CTHRC) and NASSCOM for steering the project forward and the research teams at Skills for Justice, CTHRC and AKS Consulting Services for their expertise in providing the research data which underpins this publication and the detailed sector reports.

Finally, INSSO is grateful to the specialists, without whom, this publication would not be possible in its finished form, particularly Jack Matthews, for instigating and directing the project; Trevor Boutall, Principal Consultant Partner, for his technical expertise and guidance; copy editor Tui Shaub and designer Leanor Hanny for their creative contributions; and the design team at Elmwood for their excellent work. The project team was ably supported by INSSO staff members, Emma Evans and Yenni Van, and externally, by CFE Research for details of the macro-economic analysis. We are grateful to Tom Bewick, director and chief economist, INSSO, for his advice and for writing Chapter 1.

Photographs by Mi Elfverson. Photography and illustrations by Claudia Boldt of Blunt Studios, London. All rights reserved.

NOTES
EXECUTIVE SUMMARY

[1] McKinsey Global Institute (2012) *The world at work: Jobs, pay, and skills for 3.5 billion people*, See http://www.mckinsey.com/locations/india/mckinseyonindia/pdf/MGI_Global_labor_Executive_Summary_June_2012.pdf

CHAPTER 1

[2] Mona Mourshed et al (2013) *Education to Employment* see, http://www.mckinsey.com/features/education_to_employment

[3] See, http://www.guardian.co.uk/sport/2012/oct/15/felix-baumgartner-recuperating-jump-space

[4] OECD Skills Strategy (2012) *Better Skills, Better Jobs, Better Lives: A strategic approach to skills policies*, Paris, OECD.

[5] Pisa Envy, *The Economist*, 19th January 2013, http://www.economist.com/news/international/21569689-research-comparing-educational-achievement-between-countries-growing-drawing

[6] Harrington, Ralph. *Trains, Technology and Time Travel – How the Victorians Reinvented Time*

[7] Mulgan, Geoff (2013) *The Locust and the Bee: Predators and Creators in Capitalism's*, Future Princeton University Press.

[8] Smith, Lawrence (2012) *The New North: the world in 2050*, London: Profile Books.

[9] Akerlof, George (1984) *An Economic Theorist's Book of Tales*, Cambridge University Press

[10] Brown, Phillip et al (2011) *The Global Audit: the broken promises of education, jobs and incomes.* Oxford University Press.

[11] Becker, Gary S. (1989) *Human Capital Revisited.* Ryerson lecture at the University of Chicago

[12] Becker, Gary S. (1964) *Human Capital: A theoretical and empirical analysis with special reference to education.* Third edition (1993), University of Chicago Press.

[13] Gratton, Lynda (2011) *The Shift: the future of work is already here.* London: Collins.

[14] Bewick, Tom (2013) *The Know-How Economy* See his blog at www. theknowhoweconomy.com

[15] Stephens, Dale J. (2013) *Hacking Your Education: 'Ditch the lectures, save tens of thousands, and learn more than your peers ever will.* P. 15 Pedigree, New York.

[16] McKinsey Global Institute (2012) *The world at work: Jobs, pay, and skills for 3.5 billion people,* See http://www.mckinsey.com/locations/india/mckinseyonindia/pdf/MGI_Global_labor_Executive_Summary_June_2012.pdf

[17] National Skill Development Mission (2008), see http://www.nsdcindia.org/news-events/finance-minister-meets.aspx

[18] Tulgan, Bruce (2010) *Winning the Talent Wars*, New York: W. W. Norton & Company.

CHAPTER 2

[19] 'Better skills, better jobs, better lives: A strategic approach to skills policies', OECD, Paris, May 2012

[20] These detailed reports are published separately. See, www.insso.org

[21] The Australian Workforce and Productivity Agency provides expert advice to the Australian government on the Skills Occupational List (SOL), see, http://www.awpa.gov.au/our-work/labour-market-information/skilled-occupation-list/Pages/default.aspx

CHAPTER 4

[22] ILO Global Employment Trends 2013

[23] http://skills.oecd.org/hotissues/skillsmismatch.html

[24] National Policy on Skill Development. (2009). Directorate General of Employment and Training, Ministry of Labour, India. Available on http://labour.gov.in/policy/NationalSkillDevelopmentPolicyMar09.pdf

[25] OECD, 2013, *Harnessing the Skills of Migrants and Diasporas to Foster Development: Policy Options*

[26] IOM, 2013, *Recognition of Qualifications and Competences of Migrants*

[27] *Employment and Human Resources in the Tourist Industry. International Labour Organization Sectoral Activities Programme.* 2003